GRAYSLAKE AREA PUBLIC LIBRARY
W9-BUQ-155

YOU FEEL SO MORTAL

YOU FEEL SO MORTAL

Essays on the Body

PEGGY SHINNER

The University of Chicago Press * Chicago and London

A lifelong Chicagoan, *Peggy Shinner* teaches in the creative writing MFA programs at Roosevelt and Northwestern Universities.

The University of Chicago Press, Chicago 60637
The University of Chicago Press, Ltd., London

Printed in the United States of America

23 22 21 20 19 18 17 16 15 14   1 2 3 4 5

ISBN-13: 978-0-226-10527-7 (cloth)
ISBN-13: 978-0-226-12780-4 (e-book)

DOI: 10.7208/chicago/9780226127804.001.0001

Library of Congress Cataloging-in-Publication Data
Shinner, Peggy, author.
[Essays. Selections]
You feel so mortal : essays on the body / Peggy Shinner.
pages cm
ISBN 978-0-226-10527-7 (hardcover : alkaline paper) —
ISBN 978-0-226-12780-4 (e-book) 1. Human body. 2. Body image.
3. Human body—Folklore. 4. Human body—Mythology. I. Title.
GT495.S54 2014
814′.6—dc23

2013031722

♾ This paper meets the requirements of ANSI/NISO Z39.48-1992 (Permanence of Paper).

FOR ANN

The body was like a sweet, dim dog trotting lamely toward the gate as you tried slowly to drive off, out the long driveway. *Take me, take me, too*, barked the dog. *Don't go, don't go*, it said, running along the fence . . .

LORRIE MOORE

Contents

PART ONE

Family Feet

ONE

I have, according to a dubious assemblage of pundits, propagandists, and pseudoscientists, Jewish feet. What I thought was familial is, in the eyes of some, tribal. My feet are flat. They turn out. In podiatric lingo, they pronate. *Pes planus*, in medspeak and Latin. *Liopothes*, or "people with smooth feet," wrote Greek physician Galen, who was the first to describe flat feet in the medical literature.

When I was eight or nine, my parents took me to an orthopedist. He assessed my walk, took some measurements, prescribed orthotics. I suppose I wore them, but I don't remember. I felt ashamed. Wasn't walking as natural as breathing? How could I screw up? ("It should be noted," reads an entry in Reference.com, an online encyclopedia, "that . . . horses also develop flat feet.") Already I was round-shouldered and prepubescent. Too tall. Too smart. Unathletic. I scored in the lowest percentile for the number of knee lifts I could do while hanging from the bars in gym (ten).

My feet, or more specifically my walk, seemed to be a source of family tension. I walked like my father. My mother used to say we walked like ducks. When she walked behind us, she was amused by the similarity of our turned-out gaits. Something in her amusement suggested superiority. She had high arches. Aristocratic feet. Never mind that she wore heel pads in her shoes, sorry slabs of beaten leather. Or that she and my father both came from Russian-born parents who'd fled the pogroms. Her father was a sign painter, his a tailor. Somehow she was high class and we were low. We—father and daughter—were among the fallen, the downtrodden, the miserable flat-footed. Nate Shinner and his gawky daughter, one imprinting on the other.

Over the years my feet went unreformed. And later it was my lover, not my mother, who noted them. She too seemed amused—the way you're amused, smitten almost, by the most familiar traits of the one you love. We were walking back to the car after seeing a performance of *Evita*. My father, brother, and I in front, Ann and my great-aunt behind. My father was still shaken by the image of Eva Peron's coffin being carried across the stage. His sadness annoyed me. Did he have to be so self-absorbed? Did everything have to remind him of my mother's death, even though, at the sight of the coffin, I thought of her too? My mother's life, like Eva's, prematurely occluded (Eva was thirty-three when she died, my mother fifty-six—not nearly as young as Eva, but young enough). Meanwhile, Ann, a few steps behind, had a different view. She and my aunt saw, not Eva's coffin hoisted above the shoulders of her grief-stricken followers, not Che Guevara singing "Oh What a Circus" at the edge of the crowd, but instead parent and progeny traipsing down Randolph, lock-stepped in harmony. And they were tickled. *Look at them. Can you believe it? They walk the same.* Those Shinners. Three ducks in a row. We were so endearing.

TWO

So what's Jewish about my feet, planted under my desk and swaddled, for warmth and comfort, in SmartWool? I look down at them, and even through the socks I see the rounded contours of the first joints of my big toes. The bump on my left toe is bigger. Bunions, I suppose, but they've always been there, part of my geography. Once, at a sleepover, my cousin pointed at one of them and asked me what *that* was, but I had no idea what she meant. My feet were ordinary.

Or not. History has weighed in on my body, and I have come up . . . Jewish. The evidence? Since the Middle Ages, the Jewish foot has been characterized as ugly, misshapen, flat, even cloven, like that of the he-goat and his close relative, the devil. And just as I sit here wearing socks that disguise my feet, but not really, so too have shoemakers, throughout the centuries, concealed the Jewish foot, but barely, and enabled the Jews, with their telltale feet, to pass, sort of. (Shoemaking has long been a common trade among Jews. At the turn of the twentieth century, for instance, there were 730 Jewish shoemakers in Algiers and 2,890 in London.) How do you (Jews) recognize each other? British writer Clive Sinclair was asked during a trip to Bulgaria in the early 1990s. Do you "give each other [secret] signals?" Sinclair paused for a moment before lifting his pant leg. "That's what we do," he deadpanned. "We show each other our cloven hooves."

And on it goes. English scholar and vicar Robert Burton, in his sui generis *Anatomy of Melancholy* (1621), singles out the Jew's pace, which he labels an infirmity. Johann Jakob Schudt, who chronicled the life of Jews in eighteenth-century Frankfurt, wrote of their "big heads, big mouths, everted lips, protruding eyes . . . bristle-like eyelashes, large ears, [and] crooked feet." Late nineteenth-century anatomist Hermann Schaaffhausen linked anatomy to social status and maintained that Jews walked with "the dragging gait of a lower-class individual." And Nazi caricaturist Walter Hofmann argued that because the archetypal Jew, constructed from wet clay, disobeyed divine orders and arose while the clay was still damp and soft, "the smarty developed after the first few steps extraordinary bandy legs, but also flat feet." Whereas gay men are portrayed as limp-wristed, Jewish men—often seen as effeminate and oversexed at the same time—simply limp. "Be out! Be out!" (Der muß hinaus! Der muß hinaus!), a German folk song, "Borkum Lied," exhorts anyone with "flat feet, crooked noses, and curly hair" who might dare venture to Borkum, a North Sea resort island and German vacation spot. "Out!"

Some Jews have appropriated this hobbling image, viewing it with affection. In a 2000 *GQ* article about Jewish waiters, one man fondly recalls visiting Ratner's, a deli on New York's Lower East Side, with his grandmother. "No waiters ever walked like them. They walked like they were old, even when they were 25. It was almost like they had a walker." Adds another, himself the owner of a deli in Baltimore, "They *schluffed* their feet, like they had weights on them." Apparently the Jewish waiter served up not only food but, in time-honored fashion, suffering as well.

THREE

After Schudt and Schaaffhausen and the rest, I can't help looking at my feet differently. The lens has switched. The reflection's changed. The nose, yes, there's always been the nose, but I had that fixed, didn't I? I had that dead giveaway reconfigured. The hair too—not mine, mostly straight and nondescript—but S.'s, for example, which I've long admired: dark, curly, wiry, and undeniably Semitic. But now the feet—and, it turns out, the round shoulders, the unathletic build, the odor even (*foetor judaicus*, described as "goatish" by thirteenth-century German preacher Berthold of Regensburg and "faint-sweet" by the Nazis)—all are Jewish. All have been marked, catalogued, stigmatized, labeled. Buried in the public consciousness. Once my friend J., a hospital chaplain, noted, with dawning measures of recognition and chagrin, that a rabbi she had met, with his pear-shaped body, fit a certain image she had of

Jewish men. She and Ann and I sat in her living room and nodded. We all saw it, the picture she was looking at.

I glance at my feet again. Instinctively the toes flex and then curl under. My body, under the eye of history, is off-putting. I've become a voyeur, forced to step aside and take a peek at myself. It's not front-page news that our bodies are subject to social forces. I've lived my whole life with the collective distortions of my woman's body—a faddish assemblage of parts, a repellent but tempting port of entry. And certainly women are not alone in facing such scrutiny. Blacks, for example, have long had to carry, counter, reject, ignore, or falter under the burden of their supposedly simian bodies. But I never understood my body as Jewish, a racial construction, or more to the point, a parody, and the view is unsettling. Who is this flat-footed specimen?

FOUR

Charlie Chaplin had his walk. Feet splayed, legs bowed, he walked across the twentieth century. Was it a Jewish walk? Did we, those Shinners, resemble him? He was a mustachioed man with a funny walk, who brings to mind certain images of caricatured Jews—"little Mr. Kohn," for instance, the archetypal Jew pictured on a fin-de-siècle German postcard, a lilliputian man with a top hat, cane, bowed legs, big feet. Hat, cane, feet: Chaplin and "Kohn" mirroring each other. And perhaps us Shinners too, with our flat-footed retreat from the theater after *Evita*. I once mentioned this to Ann, and she didn't dismiss the notion out of hand. A trio of ersatz Chaplins.

Charlie Chaplin, born Charles Spencer Chaplin Jr., was not Jewish. This doesn't surprise me. For one thing, and perhaps a testimony to my own provincial thinking, many Jews have a tradition of not naming their children for the living—rather, we look backward, to the dead—and there are few Jewish juniors. *The Jewish Book of Why* says that Ashkenazi Jews, in particular, "believe it would rob a person of his full life if another member of the family were to carry his name in his lifetime." In addition, records show that Chaplin was baptized in the Church of England. David Robinson, his biographer, traces his ancestry to the Huguenots. But throughout his career, Chaplin was dogged by rumors that he was Jewish, the source of which remains unclear. His surname reputedly was Thonstein. (American neo-Nazi George Lincoln Rockwell, in his book *White Power*, refers to him as Thornstein, which conveniently has embedded in it the word *horn*, another telltale sign of the Jew.) His family was said to have emigrated from eastern Europe to London in the 1850s. Chaplin himself did try some Jewish humor early in his career—at a time when Jewish comedians were popular in London—but by his own account his jokes and accent were so bad he was jeered off the stage. But then in 1940 he produced, directed, and starred in *The Great Dictator*, a bitingly funny satire of the Nazis, in which he played two roles: an unnamed Jewish barber and the dictator Adenoid Hynkel, who was modeled after Adolf Hitler. Asked if he was Jewish, Chaplin consistently refused to deny or confirm the claims, asserting that to do so would "play into the hands of anti-Semites." In the 1992 biopic *Chaplin*, starring Robert Downey Jr., a middle-aged, dapper Chaplin, accused of being a Jew on the eve of World War II, upends the slur by saying "I'm afraid I don't have that honor" before turning on his heels, linking arms with his wife at the time, actress Paulette Goddard, "the former Miss Levy" ("Levy . . . she's a Jew," an offscreen voice is heard to say), and coolly walking away.

Both Jews and anti-Semites, however, embraced the rumors. Each, in their way, claimed him (as I am now). As early as 1915, when Chaplin was twenty-six years old, a character in one of Sholem Aleichem's novels calls him "the seed of the Jews." The 1938–39 edition of *Who's Who in American Jewry*, "A Biographical Dictionary of Living Jews of the United States and Canada," lists one Charles Spencer Chaplin, motion picture actor. In 1940s Palestine, the cigarette company Kedem put out a pack of picture cards, "Images of Famous Jewish Personalities," which included Chaplin along with Albert Einstein, Max Brod, Jascha Heifetz, Lord Reading, Elisabeth Bergner, and Paul Muni. Hannah Arendt, though acknowledging that Chaplin wasn't Jewish, said his film persona "epitomized . . . a character born of the Jewish pariah mentality" and called Chaplin's Little Tramp a "little Yid." Director Sidney Lumet grew up thinking Chaplin was Jewish because he was *funny*—humor, apparently, being the special province of the Jews. In its 1937 book of photographs, *Der Ewige Jude* (The Eternal Jew), the Nazi Ministry of Propaganda oddly describes him as "flat-footed but noble." (Hitler had a soft spot for movies and the Germans had a soft spot for the Little Tramp, "who triumphs in the face of all adversaries," in the words of film critic Sabine Hake.) And the FBI, in its almost two-thousand-page dossier on Chaplin, identifies him as "Israel Thonstein," who, presumably by adopting the name of Chaplin, tried to obscure his origins and pass.

And us Shinners? We didn't pass, but perhaps we navigated a little less conspicuously, because my father and his brother, after the war and right before their respective marriages, changed their last name from the telltale Shinitzky to the more benign Shinner, and bestowed the new, assimilated moniker on their wives and soon-to-come children.

FIVE

My father's feet were ugly. Often they were bandaged. He went to the foot doctor once a month to have his calluses shaved, his corns cut out. He came home with the whole mess slathered in Mercurochrome, orange and sharp smelling like vinegar. His doctor's name was Krivit, a name whose hard sounds (so close to *divot*) suggested digging. My father called him a chiropodist, not a podiatrist, and this too seemed to reinforce the image of Dr. Krivit as an excavator, as someone who worked beneath the surface, in the underground. Chiropodist: Egyptian physician Ankmahor had one, as did Napoleon and Abraham Lincoln. Lincoln's chiropodist was a Jew named Isachar Zacharie.

Climbing into bed with my parents, my brother and I flinched at the touch of those worked-over feet. The scrape of the bandages accidentally moving across our young and as yet unmarred calves reminded us of the sores and excrescences barely covered. Was this what was in store for us? We shrieked, giddy with revulsion, and, in a flurry of bedcovers, fled.

SIX

In recent history a few celebrated Jews have been denied entry into the military. Albert Einstein, Hank Greenberg, Mel Tormé, Michael Bloomberg: all had flat feet, and all were found unfit for military service (Einstein in Switzerland), although Greenberg, initially classified as 4-F, was eventually inducted into the Army and served for four years in the Pacific during World War II. My father, flat feet notwithstanding, was sent to Mississippi for basic training. He'd never been to the South. He'd never even been out of Chicago. He grew up at the back of his father's tailor shop in Albany Park, where down the street at the little deli you could order *petcha*, calf's-foot jelly. After a few weeks at training camp, he deserted. There was a sign on an outhouse: "For dogs and jews." The other men called him hymie. (He told me this five weeks before he died, sensing, perhaps, that the game was up, and it was time to unload his secret.) His parents persuaded him to go back. They didn't want him to be rounded up. Arrested. This was the Good War. He was a good Jew. Soon he was shipped to France and wounded by shrapnel. There's a picture of him in his uniform. Dark hair. Slight smile. Private First Class Nathan Shinitzky. He looks very handsome.

SEVEN

Jews were long thought to make poor soldiers. They were weak. Cowardly. Concave-chested. The version of this that I grew up with: Jews don't fight (over the last half century, the Israel Defense Forces have put a dent in this image). Their heads are stuck in books. They were, after all, the People of the Book, mumbling away over their arcane texts. (My head *was* stuck in a book. I walked down the street bumping into light poles, reading the biographies of Amelia Earhart, Lou Gehrig, Babe Ruth. Looking up, *Excuse me*. I was no soldier. Slumped over, early breasted, and hounded home by less developed girls.) With their flat feet and gimpy gait, Jews were unsuited for the rigors of military life. Many countries excluded them from service. During the eighteenth century, for example, the Italian provinces of Sardinia-Piedmont, Parma, and Modena, as well as the Papal States, denied Jews entry into the military. When they did serve, their performance was judged substandard. An 1804 study of Jews in Austria notes that "the majority of Jewish soldiers spent more time in military hospitals than in military service" because of their weak feet. This view was so widespread that on the other side of the Atlantic, Mark Twain felt compelled to refute it. In a postscript to his 1898 article "Concerning the Jews," Twain admits that he was "ignorant—like the rest of the Christian world—of that fact that the Jew had a record as a soldier," and then he goes on to extol that record, citing Jewish participation in the Revolutionary, Mexican, and Civil Wars. But apparently Twain's new understanding did not affect the military. The 1918 US Army *Manual of Instructions for Medical Advisory Boards* claims that foreigners and "especially Jews, are more apt to malinger than the native born."

EIGHT

In the 1980 film farce *Airplane!* a stewardess walks down the aisle with a stack of magazines. She's solicitous, sexy, and helpful. She reaches up to an overhead compartment and hands someone a pillow. A nun, beatific in her expression, reads an issue of *Boys' Life*; on its cover are two boys, fishing in a stream. Meanwhile a boy, twitching with excitement, reads *Nuns' Life*, its cover featuring a nun on a surfboard, waves crashing around her, habit hiked up around her ankles.

"Do you have anything light?" an elderly passenger asks.

The stewardess flips through the magazines and pulls out a slip of paper. "How about this leaflet, 'Famous Jewish Sports Legends.'"

The audience laughs. I laugh. The idea of the Jewish athlete is laughable. Directors Jim Abrahams, David Zucker, and Jerry Zucker bank on it. Culturally savvy, they know the rap. Jews are scholars, doctors, entrepreneurs, bankers, media moguls, scientists, lawyers, and, in the case of a few poor *schlemiels*, plumbers. (Ann and I, as it happens, have a Jewish plumber. He doesn't work on the Sabbath.) But athletes? Flat feet, flabby musculature, sickly constitutions: the characteristics that have allegedly made Jews bad soldiers have made them bad athletes as well. Sandy Koufax (baseball), Mark Spitz (swimming), Lenny Krayzelburg (swimming), Sarah Hughes (skating), Sasha Cohen (skating), Kevin Youkilis (baseball)—all are mentioned in the *Jewish Sports Review*, "the Ultimate guide as to who is Jewish in the world of sports," but somehow this tribal trumpeting, with its overwrought claims ("Do you know the nine Jewish players in the NFL? Or the five in the NHL? Or the one in the NBA?") and persistent use of exclamation marks ("The Jewish Sports Review has the answers!" "Be our stringer! If you know of any professional, college, or outstanding high school Jewish athletes, please let us know!"), only serves to underscore the point that Jewish athletes are the exception rather than the rule. (I've fallen prey to such cheerleading myself, as, for instance, when the Cubs played the Milwaukee Brewers and I had to squelch the urge to tell Ann, with Brewers outfielder Gabe Kapler at the plate, *He's Jewish!* Or better yet, Jason Marquis, once a pitcher for the Cubs.) There are so few, goes the joke (in 1980, at least), that the top ones, the legends, can all fit on a single sheet of paper.

NINE

In our small backyard on Bernard Street, with a sewer cover for home plate, geraniums planted in the middle of the would-be infield, and a plum tree sprung from a pit, my father threw a sixteen-inch softball and I swung my beat-up fungo bat. Keep your eye on the ball, he advised, and we'd go back at it again. When the grass and bushes and trees converged in a veil of green and it got too dark to see, we went inside and watched the White Sox on TV. Nellie Fox and Luis Aparicio were one of the best double-play combinations in baseball.

I wasn't an athlete. I threw weakly and waywardly, in spite of my father's coaching. But I rode my bike around the neighborhood no-handed, lobbed tennis balls against the hitting wall at Northeastern Illinois University, and later, as a deluded adult, confided to a friend that when tae kwon do became an official medal event at the Olympics, I might qualify. At the time I didn't even study tae kwon do, rather a different martial art, and for only a year or two at that; but I glossed over the distinctions, not to mention the grueling years of training required of a world-class athlete, and indulged my fantasy. I suppose it's not unlike the pudgy guys who go to the Cubs fantasy camp year after year and play shortstop for a week. Or comedian Billy Crystal, who signed a one-day spring training contract with the New York Yankees, led off the game, fouled off a pitch (i.e., made contact with the ball), struck out, was replaced in the lineup by outfielder Johnny Damon, and then was released the next day, his sixtieth birthday. I wanted to be an athlete. I wanted not just to celebrate a landmark birthday with a trip to the plate but to develop a measure of physical prowess. Once I asked my friend and martial arts teacher N., whose father was a renowned swimming coach, if she'd always been physically confident, and without fanfare or false modesty, she allowed that she had. I, on the other hand, had always been fainthearted, and part of my desire to be an athlete was the desire to shed physical fear, to be free of the old restrictions.

But being an athlete was only part of the story. I wanted to *look* like one too. I wanted to turn the corner and catch a glimpse of myself, my doppelgänger, strong and assured. Years ago, when I was running regularly, a coworker's husband remarked on how athletic I looked, and I felt ridiculously pleased. Furtively I gave myself a once-over, wondering if he meant my legs. More common, however, was the reaction of the mammogram technician who, upon learning that I taught martial arts, murmured, Who would have guessed? Then she lowered the glass and flattened my breast in the machine.

"As soon as you have recognized your unathletic build, your narrow shoulders, your clumsy feet, your sloppy roundish shape," wrote Walther Rathenau, twentieth-century German statesman and himself a Jew, "you will resolve to dedicate a few generations to your renewal." Rathenau's stinging remarks were addressed to Jewish men, but he could have been talking to me. (The archetypal Jew is the male Jew; women have largely been left out of the historical record, which accounts for the dearth of female examples, although, interestingly, some stereotypical female Jewish traits—"roundish shape," "narrow shoulders"—have been attributed to the Jewish male in an attempt to feminize and thus emasculate him.) The feet, the shoulders, the build: I was the whole package, or almost (roundish but not sloppy). Instead of this Jew, Rathenau's Jew, this self-parodic image, my doppelgänger would be straighter, stronger, faster, muscled, more coordinated. She would have all her ducks in a row.

TEN

I first started martial arts because I wanted to be braver. I wanted to hitchhike across the country with élan and determination instead of staying at home like a mouse. I didn't want to be afraid of weird psychotics or creepy truckers like the one in South Dakota who gave me an axe for self-protection as I climbed out of his truck (I'd finally decided to hitchhike anyway). I thought martial arts would transform me into someone I had secretly envied in college, a woman down the hall who, as it turned out, was from Highland Park, a Chicago suburb, and heavily into drugs, but no matter. I ignored that and instead focused on her strong, sexy persona, her midlength wavy hair, her long skirts and sandals, her low-cut peasant blouses, her muscular arms, her charm, her disregard of rules, her zeal, her will, and other intangibles I couldn't possibly name then or now, invented or real. I wanted the traits she had, or imagined she had, and I thought martial arts would fix me up with them.

That was a long time ago. The Age of Aquarius has passed. I don't hitchhike anymore, but I've been studying karate for twenty years. People ask me if I can defend myself or if I can kick butt, or they put their hands up in a sign of mock surrender and say, *Well, I better not mess with you then*. But that's not why I train. I want to put my body to use. I like the structured repetition of movements, the elaborate storytelling (for instance, *kata*, or form, is a battle between two or more imaginary opponents), the compelling mix of artistry and power. I like the feeling of emptying myself out, of being spent.

Besides, I like my bravery in small doses, in increments of one hour, the duration of a karate class. Use it or lose it, my teacher has said, and she means both skills and courage, I suspect.

I step into stance. Ten kicks each leg. Palm heel, spear hand. Joint-locks, takedowns, sweeps. *Kata*s named Breaking Down the Fortress, Sound Knowledge, Big Wave, Keep Pure. Bow to your partners, the teacher says. The board breaks or it doesn't, but either way your foot tells you something when it strikes the wood. Did it hurt? somebody asks. Not if you break it.

In karate we talk about our bodies in terms of weapons and targets. Our weapons are the striking surfaces we hit with, and our targets are the areas we hit. It is language that recalls the militaristic roots of martial arts, both sobering and thrilling. Because, let's face it, there's a certain satisfaction when the weapon finds the target, as if the two were meant to come together in this synergistic way. At my black belt test, the weapon was the ball of my foot, the target two boards of one-inch pine. My goal was to propel my front kick through both boards, to split them in half. Unite with your material, my teacher once said. It felt like butter, another student commented after slipping his palm heel through a board only an inch away. I took a breath. I emptied my mind. Two students held the boards so the horizontal grain of the wood would match the oncoming trajectory of my kick, so I wouldn't be going against my material. Several practice attempts, and I was ready. Another breath. I suppose I curled back my toes and formed my weapon; launched the kick with my hips; hit the boards as hard as I could, the main advice of one of my other teachers, which, when offered, elicited laughs, because it was so obvious and resonant at the same time; I suppose I *kiai*ed—yelled—at the point of impact so my breath and technique would be coordinated, but I don't remember. I don't remember kicking or hitting the wood or going through it; I have just one lasting picture in my mind, of the boards folded in on themselves like paper, doubled over, and my foot, weapon extended, triumphantly thrust through to the other side.

ELEVEN

Pasquale Caruso was old and crippled. A plasterer by trade, he could no longer work. As he hobbled toward his Brooklyn home on the evening of March 5, 1916, a group of boys began to follow him. "Charlie Chaplin! Charlie Chaplin!" they taunted. Charlie Chaplin's tramp, in his big shoes, tight jacket, baggy pants, shuffled across the screen of every neighborhood movie house, wildly popular. But Caruso felt enraged, humiliated. The boys, he knew, were mocking him. He turned around and yelled back, shaking his fist and cursing, wondering, perhaps, how the long journey from his native Italia to the United States had come to this. After all, he had fought alongside Garibaldi to unite Italy. The boys were unfazed as they hollered and made fun of Caruso, the gimp.

Two of the boys were the sons of Joseph Certona, his neighbor. There was, one could imagine, bad blood between them. Perhaps they came from rival families back home in Italy. When Certona appeared on the corner of Fourteenth Avenue and Sixty-Sixth Street, Caruso let loose an invective against the boys and implored Certona to stop them. Instead, Certona drew a knife and slashed Caruso across the jaw.

Bloodied, Caruso staggered back to his apartment. He hauled down the old bell-mouthed shotgun he'd brought with him from Italy, not fired in over fifty years, and carried it into the hallway. Certona was waiting for him. He flashed the knife, cutting Caruso above the left eye. The two men wrestled and Certona, younger, stronger, flung Caruso to the ground. He struck at Caruso again and missed, and in that moment Caruso hoisted the shotgun and blew off Certona's head.

The stakes are high when it comes to the body. That's what I say to Ann when I tell her this story. But she points out that Certona had a knife, that one thing led to another, that the situation was not so straightforward as I would like to make it. And although I know that on one level she is right, that this may just be another tale of escalating mayhem with the usual tragic and unintended consequences, violence unleashed at one moment and out of hand the next, on another level I think of my own body, the slings and arrows I have endured, perceived, or even conjured up on its behalf—"the body, hauling sadnesses," Lorrie Moore wrote in a different context—and I hear, as I imagine Pasquale Caruso heard, the taunts of "Charlie Chaplin! Charlie Chaplin!" and think I know, if only for an instant, the shame he felt and the desire for revenge.

TWELVE

My mother and I had gone shopping at Marshall Field's. The shoe department, lingerie, Misses, Junior Miss. On the fourth floor she bought me a charm bracelet strung with pennies, which I knew I should like but didn't. I preferred the rhinestone jewelry I'd stolen from my neighbor's house but had to return. Mr. Brown, my mother had said—a shadowy person of her own invention, a kind of warden of bad children—would come and get me if I didn't give it back. We had lunch in the Walnut Room, where I ordered the Field's Special Sandwich, a mountain of iceberg lettuce, sliced turkey, Swiss cheese, bacon, and Thousand Island dressing on rye. Now we were going up the escalator, carrying packages. A man behind us, casually and contemptuously, called us kikes. He was insinuatingly intimate. There were other people on the escalator, but it was as if his taunt had cleared a space around us and now we were alone. I felt a cold, obliterating numbness. I knew what the word meant—or, in any case, I knew it meant us. My mother stiffened. I looked at the back of her long wool coat. She seemed to tell me not to look around. I was eight years old, still pudgy with baby fat. The escalator climbed to the next floor and we got off. I had to hurry to keep up with her. We went home and lived the rest of our lives: menstruation, driving lessons, depression, Vietnam. My mother died twenty years later. The rabbi read the Twenty-Third Psalm at her funeral. I'm writing this.

Pocketing

The first and last time I shoplifted, if you don't count the time I stole something from a neighbor's house—and that was a singular occurrence as well—I was in my midtwenties, living alone in a moss-green apartment across the street from the William H. Prescott Elementary School. The weekday ringing of bells marked the time. I'd hear the midmorning bell going off, the children spilling out for recess, the shrieks and scuffling, another bell, and then the capping silence as the kids lined up and squeezed back in again.

At the time I was part owner of a failing batik and tie-dye shop. This was the midseventies—*Roe v. Wade*, Nixon's resignation, the Jackson 5, Tom Wolfe's "The Me Decade." Feminists were wearing Woolrich plaid flannel shirts (I myself had several dreary favorites) and reading Eleanor Flexner's *Century of Struggle: The Woman's Rights Movement in the United States* (my copy, unfinished, still sits on the shelf); no one was interested in batik anymore. One of my business partners was a soft-spoken, dark-haired, freckled woman originally from Oklahoma whom I found earthy and ethereal at the same time. She'd coauthored a well-known book on rape. The other was a frenzied, talented, bulimic painter who had once gorged herself on a bag of flour. My credentials were less remarkable.

My theft was unremarkable too.

I suppose you could say I was young (i.e., immature), although research by the National Association for Shoplifting Prevention (NASP) indicates that a quarter of all shoplifters are between the ages of thirteen and seventeen. (In 1918, six-year-old Gretchen Grimm, the youngest of seven and the only girl, stole a lipstick at Woolworth's and gave it to her mother in an attempt, she later said, to get some attention. Grimm shoplifted into her eighties.) I was, in any case, a late or nonbloomer. I didn't do drugs (indifferent), I didn't backpack (wanted to), I didn't masturbate until I was over twenty-one and then only with the aid of a book—not something appropriately erotic, rather *Our Bodies, Our Selves*, a staple of the women's self-help movement—and I didn't have sex with someone else until I was twenty-five.

You could say I was misguided. I was in the midst of some sort of existential *Sturm und Drang* (often translated as "storm and stress," but more literally storm and urge, storm and longing, storm and drive, storm and impulse), and I stole a jar of nutmeg from the Jewel.

Where I had gone grocery shopping. Where I had, in fact, filled the cart with my small stash of weekly necessities. I was the occasional baker, and the nutmeg, I dimly reasoned, could be used in zucchini bread. I concealed the jar in my pocket, which no sooner hidden there seemed exposed, and waited in line to pay for the rest of my groceries. ("Many shoplifters buy and steal merchandise in the same visit," according to the NASP. "Shoplifters commonly steal from $2 to $200 per incident depending upon the type of store and item[s] chosen.") It was a down-at-the-heels Jewel in a modest neighborhood. Many of the shoppers were Latino. I was a diffident white woman not likely to catch anyone's attention. I left the store unnoticed.

* * *

In the nineteenth century, you might have said I was a hysteric. That's what medical and legal experts said about middle-class female shoplifters who, in fact, were not called shoplifters but kleptomaniacs. If you were lower class and stole, you were a thief. If you were middle or upper class and stole, you were sick. You *suffered* from kleptomania. Edwin S. Porter captures this class division in his 1905 film *The Kleptomaniac.* A wealthy woman goes shopping at Macy's and is caught hiding a few articles in her muff. A poor woman, desperate because she has nothing to feed her two children, steals a loaf of bread from a basket outside a shop. Both women turn up in court on the same day. The wealthy woman, head bent, crying, is exonerated, while the poor woman, castigated by the judge, is roughly led away. Lady Justice, shown in the last frame of the film, appears to peek out from her blindfold.

And the source of the kleptomaniac's illness? Like hysterics, kleptomaniacs experienced physiological disorders linked to the womb. "Women with regular or difficult pregnancies . . . irregular cycles, menopause . . . were all considered prime candidates for the designation of kleptomania," notes one historian. (Bad marriages, dead husbands, nervous conditions, ill health, and suicidal inclinations could also contribute.) With the emergence of the department store (two of the earliest were Le Bon Marché in Paris, 1838, and the Marble Place in New York, 1848, where Mary Todd Lincoln later racked up a bill of $27,000 in clothes), women, who had assumed the role of primary consumers in society, roamed aisles laden with plush silks, ivory combs, linens, handkerchiefs, stockings, and camisoles and, held hostage by their miscreant uteri, unable to control their aberrant urges, slipped a little something under their skirts. (According to the *Oxford English Dictionary*, the word *shopper* first appeared in the letters of English novelist Elizabeth Gaskell, known simply as Mrs. Gaskell, who in 1860 wrote of an acquaintance, "She is very dainty-fingered, a beautiful ready workwoman, a capital shopper.")

Take Ella Castle, for instance. On October 5, 1896, Castle and her husband Walter, wealthy American tourists, were picked up in London for shoplifting a sable muff. Because of their social status, the arrest made headlines immediately. Mrs. Castle, known in her youth for her "comeliness," had once been chosen to represent North Carolina at the Great Southern Reunion, the *New York Times* noted. Mr. Castle, a tea importer, came from a prominent San Francisco family. The US State Department rallied in their defense, as did Baron Rothschild. When London police searched their belongings at the Hotel Cecil, then the largest hotel in Europe with eight hundred rooms (and later the first headquarters for the Royal Air Force), they found, among other articles, eighteen tortoiseshell combs ("certainly in excess of their requirements"), seven ivory-framed hand mirrors, seven gold watches, seventeen fans, sixteen brooches, nine clocks, two sable boas, two neckties, and a plated toast rack and creamery jug, both bearing the Hotel Cecil stamp.

How could such thievery be reconciled with the Castles' social standing? Surely they could *buy* all these frivolities and more, if so desired. Or as their lawyer said, focusing his remarks on Mrs. Castle, "There is no reason in life why she should have taken these trumpery bits of fur." Attention zeroed in on her mental status. "Mrs. Castle is very much depressed." "Mrs. Castle has been suffering from acute headache and a feeling of intense fatigue, although she has not undergone any exertion." "She was laboring under the effects of a disease which was likely to lead to a temporary overthrow of her mind." "No doubt . . . she is a kleptomaniac." (Didn't we once fling that as a schoolyard taunt: *You're a klepto!*) Her "condition . . . has been a pathetic secret among her acquaintances for many years." "Her defense . . . would be mental irresponsibility, owing to her sufferings from troubles peculiar to females."

Female Troubles. That was the root of Mrs. Castle's behavior, the underlying cause of her sticky fingers. (The catchall phrase, used to suggest myriad reproductive-related conditions, came into common usage in the 1930s: "It's the female trouble," says Dewey Dell, seventeen years old and pregnant, in Faulkner's *As I Lay Dying*.) Mrs. Castle pled guilty to kleptomania, that quintessential female malady, while her husband "was exonerated from all responsibility for her pilferings." She was released into his care (echoes of custody), and they immediately sailed back to the United States, where she entered Philadelphia Polytechnic Hospital. There doctors diagnosed hysteria, irregular periods along with other uterine abnormalities, and hemorrhoids. She had surgery. "The sphincter ani [was] dilated, the fissures cauterized . . . the ulcers treated . . . and the hemorrhoids clamped and cauterized. The uterus was curetted and then the trachelorrhaphy [suture of the cervix] performed . . . with silkworm gut."

The records don't indicate if her kleptomania ever resurfaced.

* * *

According to some experts, kleptomania derived, not from uterine disease, but from thwarted female sexuality. Call it uterine greed. Mis- or displaced sexual voracity.

Light-fingered women needed, or wanted, a roll in the hay. But if they were unmarried? If their husbands were impotent or uninterested? If social mores prohibited extramarital partners? Then they donned their hats and gloves and went shopping. This view was put forth in fin-de-siècle France as doctors studied the phenomenon of department store thieves. Psychiatrist Roger Dupouy took note of a particularly excitable woman, who reported: "When I grab some silk, then I am just as if I were drunk. I tremble . . . I only think of one thing: to go into the corner where I can rustle it at my ease, which gives me voluptuous sensations even stronger than those I feel with the father of my children." (Psychiatrist and painter Gaëtan Gatian de Clérambault dubbed this sartorial fetish "silk erotomania.")

In his article "The Sexual Root of Kleptomania," published in the *Journal of the American Institute of Criminal Law and Criminology* (1911), Dr. Wilhelm Stekel, a Viennese psychologist and early follower of Freud, zeroes in on the impulse that "suddenly compelled [a woman] to touch some object and *put it in her pocket*" (italics Stekel's). He explains the dynamic in this way:

> These women fight against temptation. They are engaged in a constant struggle with their desires. They would like to do what is forbidden, but they lack the strength. Theft is to them a symbolic act. The essential point is that they do something that is forbidden, *touch* something that does not belong to them.

Afterward—i.e. the proverbial morning after—some women can't remember what happened; others are ashamed; some refuse to touch the stolen object.

And what did these women steal? Stockings, furs, gloves, bags, bracelets, rings—all articles, Stekel points out, into which something was put—that is, ersatz sexual orifices; umbrellas which, when opened, suggested erect penises; and in one case, a music box, representative of a servant's "homo-sexual desire to play with the genital parts of her mistress."

* * *

We had a plastic radio on the kitchen counter, next to the Osterizer, and at nine or ten I found myself caught between two songs: "Around the World" (from the 1956 film *Around the World in 80 Days*) on the one hand and "Que Sera, Sera" (also from a 1956 film, Hitchcock's *The Man Who Knew Too Much*) on the other. I wanted to tag along with Nat King Cole, to "New York or gay Paree or even London Town," an offer he made liltingly appealing; but at that point in my life I'd gone no further than Nippersink, a washed-out resort just over the border in Wisconsin, and the prospects for a more far-reaching life seemed dim. So there was Doris Day instead, singing cheerfully (if not convincingly) of sacrifice and acceptance—"Whatever will be, will be / The future's not ours to see / Que sera, sera"—and although the song had a certain appeal to the latent martyr in me (the romance of suffering and surrender), I also felt the weight of its dreary resignation. (Today I can't hear the Serenity Prayer, a homily of contested origin sometimes attributed to theologian Reinhold Niebuhr and later adopted by AA and other 12-step programs—"God grant me the serenity to accept the things I cannot change; courage to change the things I can; and wisdom to know the difference"—without bristling at its buck-up note of acquiescence and relinquishment.) And confirming my fear of a life writ crampingly small, possibilities quashed or diminished, there were my mother's words, said years later in a moment of pique and anger, when my choices weren't lining up with hers: *Happiness isn't everything.*

* * *

I don't know why I took a jar of nutmeg. It seemed like some sort of test. Was I daring enough? Brave enough? Bad enough? I wanted to be transgressive, and although I had come out a year before, apparently being a lesbian—or *identifying* as one, the term used in the seventies, the heyday of identity politics—wasn't transgressive enough, not when I'd been too chicken to actually initiate sex. (Oh, maybe like Dr. Stekel said, I just needed to put something in my pocket.) I wanted to get away with something. Perhaps I wanted to get away with being someone other than myself. Nutmeg, of course, is a spice, at one time highly sought after and expensive, and dare I say, at the risk of being embarrassingly simplistic, that when I stole a jar of nutmeg, I stole a bit of exoticism, a little pizzazz to spruce things up? (Nutmeg: aromatic, medicinal, poisonous, narcotic. Its fragrance perfumed the streets of Rome in honor of Henry VI's coronation as Holy Roman Emperor. Arab physicians claimed it was an aphrodisiac; the English used it as an abortifacient. Malcolm X took it to get high in prison. "Stirred into a glass of cold water, a penny matchbox full of nutmeg had the kick of three or four reefers." "You don't ever want someone to taste something and say, 'Oh: nutmeg,'" Julia Child said.) Well, okay. I wanted to liven things up. Once I'd cheated during an exam at school by deliberately dropping a pencil so I could get up, retrieve the bait, and sneak a look at the paper of the kid in front of me, and the whole episode seemed as much about actually having the guts to cheat as it did about getting the right answer. I didn't want to end up like my fifth-grade teacher Miss Tubin, who, with her quavering timidity, big bosom, Peter Pan collars, buckteeth, was the laughingstock of all the students.

Instead of transgressive, I was responsible. In high school I was voted Most Industrious in my senior class, which carried, to me, a hint of drudgery. At the batik shop K., in good humor, gave us taglines, labels supposedly reflecting our essential traits, and although I don't remember the others, mine was "reliable." I smiled and bore it dutifully, but deep down it felt like an unintended barb, like being called a journeyman ballplayer: good enough to go from team to team but not good enough to star on one. And later, when my mother was dying, she confided she wasn't worried about what would become of me, she was worried about my brother—never as industrious or reliable, a bit of a ne'er-do-well (who eventually moved to San Francisco and, like Walter Castle, became a successful tea importer)—and I desperately, childishly, craved her concern. *Worry about me.*

* * *

It was envy that led me up the stairs of my neighbor's house to take a handful of costume jewelry. I was about seven or eight. We didn't have anything like this. My mother didn't wear rhinestones. They were gaudy, unrefined, low class. The neighbors lived five houses down in a Georgian. We lived in a ranch. I was envious that they got to sleep on the second floor, while we slept on the first. They went somewhere when they went to bed. They saw the stars. We just went to bed. I snuck into a second-floor bedroom to steal the jewelry.

The mother and daughter were redheads. L.'s hair was brassy. She wore housecoats and flowered muumuus and red toenail polish. Her daughter R.'s hair was orange and unruly. She had a gravelly voice and was exuberant and fat. Her father was some kind of city hack.

My mother found the jewelry, and made me give it back. She was unyielding. She refused to intercede with the Pickards. She said if I didn't return the jewelry, she would call Mr. Brown and he would punish me. Mr. Brown, a boogeyman she had conjured up to frighten me into compliance. What child wouldn't be afraid of a lurking man who took off with misbehaving children? Does everyone have a Mr. Brown? Someone whose mere mention and dark-sounding name curb aberrant behavior and subdue one into submission? Mr. Brown might have been summoned, but he never came.

* * *

Relief, triumph, letdown.

Now I was a person who shoplifted. I walked from the Jewel back to my apartment two blocks away. Past the school, the empty playground. The children were all tucked inside their classrooms. The bells were silent. I'd gotten away with something. I'd gotten away with taking something that didn't belong to me but seemed to belong to other people: women who hitchhiked across the country, waded in tide pools and pried mussels off the rocks for dinner, tramped through the Three Sisters Wilderness, were bisexual and then carted out the lovers to prove it. I was no longer the good girl who, as a child, apologized when she bumped into a light pole on the street. I was, looking at the jar of nutmeg on my kitchen table, a thief. A shoplifter. A klepto!

I imagine it this way, but in fact I don't remember. Did I feel, like my French counterpart almost a century before, "voluptuous sensations"? Did I wave the jar under my nose, reveling in the fragrance (medieval Romans called it *nuce muscāta*, "musk-smelling nut")? In the store, with the nutmeg burning a hole in my pocket, I couldn't wait to make my escape. But beyond the relief of avoiding disclosure or arrest, I don't remember what I did or felt, or if I felt anything. My foray into crime left nothing in its wake. I never stuck out my thumb to get to Oregon and climb the Three Sisters. I did eat mussels off the rocks for dinner once, yes, but someone else tore them loose and steamed them. There were no lovers waiting in the wings. I was back across the street from the Prescott School, with a few more ounces of *nuce muscāta* in the pantry.

All these years later, I feel embarrassed about the nutmeg. Telling my friends N. and S. about it, I laugh, apologetically, so they won't laugh first. My theft was so puny. I'd wanted to make a grand statement, stride across on the big stage (Helen Reddy–ish and roaring), but I wasn't a good shoplifter, just like I wasn't a good cheat. Brave enough to take something, but not enough to do it with panache. When the pressure was on (self-imposed), all I took was an ounce of spice, which today costs $4.75 and then even less. Not long ago, I saw that familiar bumper sticker on a car at the gym: "Well-behaved women seldom make history," and in one of those moments when everything seems to converge, when a slogan becomes a comment on your character, I took it as a coda to my shoplifting. The slogan was originally from an essay by historian Laurel Thatcher Ulrich about Puritan women, and later appropriated for mugs, T-shirts, magnets, buttons, and greeting cards (the Sweet Potato Queens, a rollicking group of women from Jackson, Mississippi, sold their tee along with another that read "Never Wear

Panties to a Party") before being reclaimed by Ulrich herself as the title for one of her books. At its heart, Ulrich's slogan questions an overly pedantic adherence to social mores. *See*, I thought, as if one part of me had been in a long-standing argument with another, and now, with the bumper sticker chiming in, the dispute was over. Too polite, too well behaved, too cautious, I'd hardly made a splash.

* * *

Time to talk about sex. I've alluded to it, avoided it, joked about it, thumbed my nose at it (or, in any case, at the messengers, Wilhelm Stekel and his French cohorts), and pined away for it. Now it's time to drop the evasions. Shoplifting and sex. The relationship, if any, between theft and desire. I laughed when I first read Dr. Stekel's analysis. But in considering my brief flirtation with shoplifting, I have repeatedly put the two together. I've made note of my sexual history on the same page that I described slipping the nutmeg into my pocket. Was Stekel onto something when he said, "Theft is to them [meaning kleptos] a symbolic act"? Or even more explicitly, Dr. Fritz Wittels, when he wrote in the *Journal of Criminal Psychopathology* (1942), "To steal is actually the sex life of Kleptomaniacs"? I've avoided addressing these theories, in part because they're ridiculous. They reflect a deep fear and disgust of female sexuality. Female desire is dangerous, illicit, uncontrollable. It is a mania, a source of social disorder, which can only be understood, and perhaps contained, in the context of illness, crime, and, alas, commerce. Reduced to a kinky transaction.

And although these ideas have been largely abandoned (there are some diehards, like Dr. Marcus J. Goldman, who as recently as 1998 maintained, "Kleptomania, with its excitement and risk, likely serves as a transition between mature sexuality and a more primitive self-gratifying behavior or stance") and kleptomania is now classified as an impulse control disorder in the *Diagnostic and Statistical Manual of Mental Disorders*, a part of me is afraid they might be true. Did I steal the nutmeg as a substitute for sex? Was the desire to be transgressive really the desire to fulfill desire? Did I just need a little nookie? Well, I did need a little nookie, there's no denying that. I was waiting in the wings to be discovered. As a teenager, in one of those dimly lit basement sessions with friends when everyone confesses something, I'd said rather brashly, with some intent to shock, that if I found out I had six months to live, I'd want to have sex before I died. A grand denouement. An exultant exit plan.

But shoplifting wasn't sex. Shoplifting was, in its aftermath, a paltry and inconsequential act. I did not, in the words of one of Dr. Wittels's patients, "feel a wild triumph, a lust the like of which nothing else can offer." I had no urge to do it again, even though it would be a year or so before someone, finally, in the green-walled apartment across from the school, led me to bed. Shoplifting's a rite of passage, a friend said in her direct, matter-of-fact way. (A common-enough observation, with numbers to back it up: according to the NASP, 89 percent of teens say they know other teens who shoplift.) Her hands rested on her loose-fitting wine-colored tie-dyed top, which, reminiscent of the late sixties, could have come from my long-ago defunct shop. Didn't everybody do it? she asked. (And in this way I suppose you could say it does resemble sex.) First I felt a jolt of surprise, almost of chagrin, as if I'd been taken down a notch or two—as if some hidden core of self-exceptionalizing had unwittingly been revealed—before being swept up by the easy candor of her comments and the details, much more remarkable than mine, of her own rowdy exploits.

Debutante, Dowager, Beggar

I was a Dr. Spock baby. My mother kept *The Pocket Book of Baby and Child Care* in the end table next to the couch in the living room, where I found it once when I was looking through drawers for evidence of family secrets, a favorite childhood pastime, and where it remained until two years after her death, when my father decided to sell the house and move to an apartment. Periodically I would open this drawer and take out the book and idly flip through the pages. What did it tell me about my mother, or my mother about her children? My mother, a binge eater, insecure cook, sharp dresser (dressed to kill, a friend's mother once said, with equal parts malice and envy), and the family ledger-keeper and handyperson, who often seemed daunted by the rigors of raising children. She died in her midfifties, a woman about whom you might have predicted an early death, perhaps because she seemed afraid of life and gave off a persistent whiff of unhappiness. "Use the Index at the back when you are troubled," Dr. Benjamin Spock suggested, and I imagine her folded in the corner of the couch, legs tucked under her housecoat, a Marlboro in the ashtray on the end table. It was late at night. My father was snoring ballistically from the bedroom. The house seemed to be ticking with worry.

My mother turned to the calm, soothing Spock for advice. Here, between "Port-wine stains" and "Potato, gagging on," was the problem: "Posture." "Bad posture is made up of a number of factors," Spock wrote in the Pocket Book edition first published in 1946 and in its twentieth printing by 1951, the year I was born. These factors included genetics ("individuals who [are] round-shouldered . . . like their fathers before them," a trait, it turns out, that historically has been used to characterize large swaths of people, in particular the Jews, and has even made it into the stockpile of contemporary Jewish humor, as evidenced by this joke about Zen Judaism: "Let your mind be as a floating cloud. Let your stillness be as the wooded glen. And sit up straight. You'll never meet the Buddha with such rounded shoulders"), disease (rickets, infantile paralysis), obesity, psychology ("many children slouch because of lack of self-confidence"), "unusual tallness" (which, presumably, leads to efforts to conceal it by slouching). Whatever the cause, nagging your child to "stand up straight!" didn't work. Instead, Spock recommended a more reasoned approach: "posture work at school, in a posture clinic, or in a doctor's office." The parents' job, he emphasized—his persistent, persuasive voice insinuating itself into the consciousness of 1950s middle-class America—was to "help the child's spirit by . . . making him feel adequate and self-respecting."

* * *

Excellent (A). Good (B). Poor (C). Bad (D). These were the broad posture categorizations first established in 1926 by the Children's Bureau, a federal agency under the US Department of Labor, and still being referred to by body mechanics specialists over twenty-five years later, during my childhood. I had bad posture. My parents' concern was corroborated by an unwaveringly upright, six-foot-tall, fourth-grade teacher who wore straight skirts that accentuated her bearing and who told me to pull my shoulders back. I was a slumper, a sloucher. I had round shoulders. The Children's Bureau illustrated the four categories with silhouettes of naked children in increasingly slumping postures and defined Bad (D) by these characteristics: "head markedly forward; chest depressed (sunken); abdomen completely relaxed and protuberant; back curves extremely exaggerated." And what was the corrective? The twentieth century saw the rise of an organized posture movement in the United States that was led by the American Posture League in the early part of the century, and taken up by both medical and educational professionals throughout the country. Bad posture, according to these experts, contributed to a variety of problems, including backache, vomiting, colitis, constipation, menstrual irregularity, heart disease, tuberculosis, organ displacement, hernia, and mental impairment, and was a symbol of moral weakness in both individuals and the culture at large. Children were exhorted by means of slogans, plays, poems, and songs to stand up straight, and many received posture training in school or were referred to posture clinics (as Dr. Spock advocated) for treatment. In the 1950s, Posture Paul, "the streetcar that knows good posture," offered himself up as an example. In a record meant to inspire Los Angeles public schoolchildren, but whose message was apt for slumping children everywhere, Posture Paul, singing to the tune of Stephen Foster's "Oh! Susanna," kept his "feet straight on the track," "push[ed his] cushion back," "tucked [his] tummy in," "held his chest high and shoulders soft," and then, in a final verse punctuated by the streetcar's clanging, promised,

> If this advice you take from me
> And always wear a smile
> You will grow to be a healthy child
> And live a long long while.

* * *

I'm a part-time self-defense teacher. In class, the students sculpt each other into statues. This is aggressive, they say. Passive. Assertive. The aim of the exercise is to examine various behaviors and their physical manifestations, and to explore how self-presentation might impact the outcome of a situation. The aggressive statues have their hands in fists, their faces set in a mock attempt to look fierce or threatening, their bodies lunging forward. They take up lots of room, like the man next to you on the bus whose body heedlessly crowds yours. The passive statues are turned in on themselves, eyes down, shoulders hunched or narrow. The assertive statues project confidence, assuredness, shoulders square, feet planted, eyes focused, neither threatening nor timid. It's a balance beam, I say, in a worn but handy metaphor. If the beam tips one way or the other, we can always right it. We are an ever-evolving work in progress.

But I'm uneasy. In my stylishly gray T-shirt with THINK/YELL/RUN/FIGHT/TELL—the five fingers of self-defense—in bright, block primary colors like Legos, which make self-defense look like a game anyone would want to play, I'm an advertisement for cheery self-empowerment. And yet as I say these things—we want to be on the assertive part of the balance beam—and look at these stiffly comical and by now tottering totems of behavior (the students laugh, self-conscious but intrigued by the exercise too), I feel dishonest. A tattletale, pointing the finger at my own slumped self. I'm exposing my highly visible secret. If the students haven't seen me—that is, tagged me as someone with bad posture—if I haven't yet given myself away, surely they've seen this representation, the statue with the round shoulders. The hunched back. My cover, if I ever had one, is gone.

Do we ever know what we look like? Perhaps we recognize ourselves in others, but do we recognize ourselves in ourselves? Pinned on the bulletin board in her study, Ann has a baby picture of me in which my neck is craned, my lips pursed, and she says that the expression I have in that photo, which she mimics by working her own lips like a hungry chick's, is the same I have in certain whimsical moments now, at sixty. But of course I don't see it. I'm blind to myself. Just like I'm blind to the person whose reflection tags along with me in store windows. (Look at yourself in store windows, physical educator Ivalclare Sprow Howland recommends in her 1936 book, *The Teaching of Body Mechanics*: "'To see ourselves as others see us' is profoundly important in taking personal inventory of one's bodily attitudes.") Occasionally I'll sneak a look at her as I pass by, as if stealth itself has the power to catch her unawares. But I'm the one caught unawares. The person I see, with her head forward and back curved, surprises me. I turn away.

* * *

Meet Adrelene. She's my doppelgänger. She's featured in the 1953 educational film *Your Posture*, made by Centron Corporation in consultation with the School of Public Health at the University of California. The opening scene is a party. Girls and boys playing musical chairs. They're eleven or twelve years old. The girls in shirtwaists and pageboys. The boys in jackets and ties, buzzed hair. Betty Brant's at the piano, "the kind of girl who puts life in a party," the voice-over says. And "Jimmy and Sue and Jean and the rest of the gang" are all having a wonderful time. All except Adrelene. Adrelene circles the chairs, head down, eyes darting. She looks nervous, mousy. First round, she gets eliminated. She slinks off by herself. "Adrelene," the voice-over says, heavy with pity and regret. "Adrelene," he repeats—so the oddness of her name and the direness of her situation sink in—"who usually sits slumped in her chair in the corner." Outsider name, outsider status. The other kids laugh at her. She doesn't fit in. "Your posture is your problem," he continues. And then, half threat, half challenge, "What are you going to do about it?"

This was the 1950s, when the posture movement still held sway. Posture Queen contests were staged all over the country, young women in bathing suits and high heels posing next to life-size x-rays of their spines. One photo from 1957 shows Miss Michigan in a strapless bathing suit, legs demurely crossed, sitting on top of a light box displaying her illuminated spine and pelvis while she holds a trophy and wears a crown. Barnard College held a posture contest for freshmen every January, during which, according to *Life* magazine, "circling contestants walk[ed] for half an hour, rather like entrants in a live stock show." In Seattle there was a posture contest for preschoolers. The governors of Maryland, Minnesota, Arkansas, Kansas, and Kentucky all signed proclamations for Posture Week. The Arthur Murray dance studio in New Orleans sponsored a good-posture dancing demo.

And what about Adrelene? In the heyday of the posture movement, it was apparently permissible, indeed laudable, to deride someone for her posture as a means of goading her to improve. Social ostracism and self-flagellation were part of the prevailing ethos. First the kids at the party send her heading off to the corner; then at home Adrelene's mirror image turns against her and mocks the way she carries herself. "Do you want to see how you really look, Adrelene? This is it. Your head pokes forward, your shoulders slump, your stomach—well, take a look" (echoes of the Children's Bureau 1926 description). At first Adrelene is stricken, but then she rallies. She's gonna beat this rap. She shakes a finger at the mirror. "Atta girl, Adrelene."

Also part of the prevailing ethos, as evidenced by the film, is that kids are in charge here. They are the enforcers. They mete out the punishment. In the opening scene, there's hardly an adult in sight, except the party chaperone hovering on the fringes, rounding up the kids for a game of musical chairs. And later, when Adrelene's back at home and in front of her rogue mirror, her parents are oddly absent as well. (Perhaps they're missing because if they had known what had gone on at the party, they might have been outraged on their daughter's behalf.) Only later, after the kids have done their job, do the adults appear. Dr. Martin comes to Adrelene's classroom to lecture on the fundamentals of good posture, and the film changes its focus from social ostracism to instruction.

Kids as enforcers: that was long one of the themes of the posture movement, and a teaching strategy advocated by educators such as Ivalclare Sprow Howland. "Do [students] report recognizing poor body mechanics in others?" she asked, implying that they should. At Battle Creek College, where Howland was an associate professor, "student coaches in Body Mechanics" wrote *The Slump Family*. In this play, intended for use with grammar-school-aged children, the Slump children arrive home from school and teach Mother and Daddy Slump a new song, to the tune of "Frere Jacques"/"Brother John":

> Perfect Posture, perfect posture
> Do not slump, do not slump;
> You must grow up handsome,
> You must grow up handsome,
> Hide that hump, hide that hump.

Stand "like the Indians do," the children say, demonstrating proper alignment to their pepless mother and headachy father—whose boss at the factory has just threatened to fire him if he doesn't shape up (fatigue and general ill health being the result of poor posture)—and then "we won't . . . be the Slump Family anymore."

Howland also suggested that children be enlisted as "posture cops," a peer-monitoring activity suitable for Good Body Mechanics and Posture Week. In this game, the kid cops tag classmates who exhibit good posture. Such games, wrote design historian Carma R. Gorman,

> were clearly intended to develop a culture of surveillance in order to enforce properly disciplined carriage. . . . Both official and unsanctioned monitoring activities communicated to stu-

dents not only that they were being constantly watched and judged based on their form, but also that they should in turn feel free—even obligated—to judge the health, efficiency, and character of others.

American Posture League founder Jessie Bancroft once noted, seemingly with approval, that "the boys in one class waylaid a classmate after school and pommeled him because his poor posture kept the class from one hundred per cent."

This culture of surveillance wasn't limited to kids. In the 1920s, during Posture Week at Vassar, students who had passed a posture test secretly observed their fellow students for two weeks, graded them on their carriage, and passed the results on to the instructors. Designated Posture Police, they wore badges with the insignia S.U.S.—Stand UP Straight—and lined up in two rows outside the recitation hall each morning, where, in a cross between a military drill and a police lineup, the other students had to walk between them. Students even upbraided trees, admonishing them with placards "to hold themselves straight."

* * *

I was, as Dr. Spock suggested, unusually tall. In kindergarten I asked the teacher why I was so tall and my classmate, R., so short. There's a picture of me from around that time, next to my brother in a baby buggy, in which I already look like a beleaguered housewife. My dress is rumpled, I'm snarling at my brother, and slumping.

Again my parents took me to an orthopedist. This time I was ten. I dressed up for the appointment in a shirtwaist. After the examination and the x-rays, the evidence of my errant spine slapped up on a screen, he recommended a brace. In a rare act of defiance, I refused. A brace would make me a freak. Instead we were sent home with a set of exercises and the grim sense that I better do them.

I did do them. For one of the exercises, I lay on the floor in my parents' bedroom while my mother held down my ankles. Her weight bore into me as I arched my back and lifted my upper body off the floor. This was supposed to strengthen my back muscles. (The exercise derived from the Kraus-Weber tests, six measurements of physical fitness developed in the 1940s and '50s at the Posture Clinic of Columbia-Presbyterian Hospital in New York. The poor performance of American schoolchildren on these tests eventually led to the establishment of the President's Council on Youth Fitness in 1956.) But to be down on the carpet with her, an intimacy I found mortifying, to be cajoled and restrained, her hands clamped around my ankles, to be laughed at when I accidentally let out some gas, was humiliating. Maybe, in the end, she hated it too. Over time I stopped the exercises altogether.

* * *

In 1632 Dutch poet and statesman Constantijn Huygens noticed that the head of his four-year-old son, Constantijn Jr., leaned to the left. Concerned, the father tried "a stiff collar, ribbons attached to his bonnet, [and] . . . steaming his neck . . . to no avail." Huygens considered taking his son to a local peasant, a bonesetter of notorious reputation, but finally opted for a university-trained physician from Utrecht instead. The doctor "made a gash of two inches long in the poor boy's neck, separating . . . the many entangled sinews there and greasing the whole machinery with some oil." The operation was deemed a success. The boy's posture was righted, and he eventually went on to a career as the personal secretary of Prince William III, the future king of England.

* * *

Upstanding, upright, upscale, straightforward, straightaway, high-minded, high-spirited, stand-up, stand fast, stand tall, take a stand.

Crook, crooked, bowed, befallen, bent out of shape, in a slump, downtrodden, downsize, cut down to size, down and out, low-down, laid low.

We have a whole vocabulary built around posture. It suggests that standing tall stands head and shoulders above slouching; that to slouch belies, indeed violates, a moral imperative deeply embedded in our culture. Slumping isn't just ugly or bad for your health; it diminishes your entire being. In its various guises (the huddled masses, the beggar, the supplicant, the criminal, the baseball player who can't buy a hit), it suggests a lessening of selfhood, a reduction of power. Heterosexuals are straight; homosexuals are bent. ("He's a bit bent," says Max, a fact about himself he's loath to acknowledge, so he couches it in the third person, in Martin Sherman's 1979 play *Bent*, set in Nazi Germany.) The name Obama, in Dholuo, the language of the Luo from western Kenya, means "crooked or bent," which some Obama detractors latched on to during the 2008 presidential election as evidence of his innate untrustworthiness. Posture reflects personality, according to educators in the posture movement: "Sneaky people, cowards, and criminals all could be identified by their bad posture." Take a look at Dr. Jekyll, one educator instructed—upright and noble, in contrast to Mr. Hyde, crouching and evil. Your Highness, an honorific bestowed on royalty, is the top dog in a top-down hierarchy. "You're the top!" goes the Cole Porter song. "I'm a worthless check, a total wreck, a flop / But if, baby, I'm the bottom you're the top!"

* * *

Has your back always been like this? a massage therapist once asked me, seemingly without hesitation, as if because she was running her hands all over me, my body were fair game for discussion. Music drifted in the background. Her hand moved along my back, like she was tracing a curiosity, committing it to memory. She almost seemed to regard this slip of spine with absentminded affection.

Has my posture always been like this? French sociologist Marcel Mauss, in his groundbreaking *Techniques of the Body* (1934), argues that our body movements emerge from a host of sociological, biological, and psychological factors. They are not only fixed in the individual; they are part of the culture. Or, in the words of twentieth-century philosopher-anthropologist Pierre Bourdieu, "The body is in the social world but the social world is also in the body." For the ancient Greeks, a crooked head marked a slave, an erect head a free man. For Dr. Eliza Mosher, professor of hygiene, sanitation, and home economics at the University of Michigan in the late nineteenth century and a leading proponent of the posture movement, the "general body shape of idiots and defectives as compared with those of normal powers indicate a close relation between a lack of brain development and . . . posture." For Vassar's physical education director in 1930—the height of the eugenics movement, when posture standards could be used to weed out the less than upright—"inadequate" posture was cause for student dismissal. My parents' concern likely came down to looks, and its consequences. They felt, I suspect, a combination of pity, alarm, distaste, and disapproval. I was their Adrelene. Bad enough that bad posture was unattractive (Emily Post, that maven of etiquette, put it this way: "A round-shouldered slouch . . . certainly does little to make one appealing"); it could condemn one to social ostracism, and worse yet, in the unforgiving economy of the marketplace, render a woman unmarriageable as well.

* * *

Call someone a slouch, and the word, according to the *Oxford English Dictionary*, conjures "an awkward . . . or ungainly [person]; a lubber, lout, clown; also, a lazy, idle fellow," just as it has since its origins in the sixteenth century. Francis Grose's *A Classical Dictionary of the Vulgar Tongue* (1785) characterizes a slouch as "negligent" and "slovenly." In a letter to Henry James, Robert Louis

Stevenson wrote, "I recognise myself, compared with you, to be a lout and slouch of the first water." George Eliot, in *Scenes of Clerical Life*, describes one of the street characters as an idiot "slouching along with a string of boys at his heels." A slouch has always had a bad rep.

Enter the "debutante slouch," circa 1913. (The phrase is listed in the Library of Congress's 1913 *Catalogue of Copyright Entries*.) This is a slouch of a different order. It has pedigree. It comes from a storied line of class and money. A high-society knockoff reputedly named for the walk of upper-class women, the debutante slouch made its way across a rapidly changing American landscape. In a spirit of freedom and rebellion, women of all classes took it on: "shoulders sloping, chest dropped, hips slung forward and the knees (in more pronounced cases) slightly bent." As etiquette manuals had long noted, the way you walked said something about you. It was

> an index of [your] character . . . [your] culture . . . [your] frame of mind. . . . There is the thoughtful walk and the thoughtless walk, the responsible walk and the careless walk, the worker's walk and the idler's walk, the ingenuous walk and the insidious walk, and so on.

With their sinuous posture, women who adopted the debutante slouch emphasized the relaxation of all kinds of strictures. They were no longer bound by the old standards of modesty, deference, and decorum. They abandoned their corsets; marched down Fifth Avenue demanding the right to vote; took over jobs as elevator operators, drawbridge attendants, and train dispatchers during World War I; drank Gibsons; and had sex.

But the slouch had its detractors. Doctors cited the usual list of medical mishaps that could result, including organ prolapse, for which, as treatment, one prominent Houston surgeon went so far to suggest

> two to three months in bed with the foot of the bed elevated 18 inches . . . a well regulated fattening diet . . . daily massage and attention to the bowels followed by twelve months use of correctly fitting front lace corset . . . before [an] operation should be required.

For others an upright posture was a religious imperative. One commentator in the Lowville, New York, *Journal and Republican* said God made man upright, unlike the four-legged creatures, and therefore he must bear himself like a king. Not to do so was to court God's displeasure and bring on "evil consequences." Some critics saw the slouch as a sign of moral turpitude, a racial marker differentiating the proud white woman from the African American. On a visit to an all-girls' New York City high school in 1914, General George W. Wingate, cofounder of the National Rifle Association, castigated the students for adopting this new posture. "You girls walk a lot like slaves," he said. "There is nothing of the queenly pose, the power, the upright carriage, which ought to mark free-born women. When I see our young women walking on the street I am ashamed of our race." This link to race was echoed in the remarks of a fashion commentator who noted it was one thing when a sixteen-year-old with a girlish figure affected the debutante slouch, but another when a forty-year-old tried it. No longer young and winsome, she risked looking like a "negro mammy with her bundle of washing." Finally, and quite simply, one critic for the *Pittsburgh Press* said, "Slouching is so ugly!"

* * *

The cover illustration of the December 5, 2005, issue of the *New Yorker* depicts then president George Bush and vice president Dick Cheney in their joint quarters at the White House. The room is a mess. A picture tilts precariously on the wall, a partially eaten piece of pizza sits on a plate; dishes, flatware, a teacup, empty beer cans litter the floor. Bush is neatly dressed in a shirt, tie (complete with tie clip), and khakis. One hand rests on his hip; the other holds a feather duster. A carefully folded dish towel hangs from his waistband; the red stripe on the towel echoes the red of his tie. His head tilts to the side, his posture is subtly slouched, and he's staring out of the frame, looking irritable, flummoxed, and petulant all at once. *Can you believe this place?* his expression seems to say.

Cheney, for his part, is sprawled in a chair. His feet are splayed atop a map on the coffee table, shoelaces untied; his shirt cuffs are open, his tie undone. The smoke of his cigar trails off like an inscrutable thought bubble. There's a newspaper section in his hand, on his lap, and under the chair on the floor. He's not reading the paper, though. His eyes are focused elsewhere, as though he's mulling over what he just read. His mouth twists to the side in consideration.

This cover raises an issue frequently bandied about during the Bush years: Who held the real power? Was Bush in control, or was he the front man for the often behind-the-scenes Cheney, who, with his ties to Halliburton, his longtime defense background, and his stringently ideological and aggressive personality, was actually running the show? In the visual vocabulary of the the *New Yorker* illustration, was it fastidious George or sloppy Dick? The tight-lipped slumper or the big-chested guy draped across the width of the page? There are many signifiers in this illustration, chief among them postural ones. As Adam Galinsky, professor of ethics and decisions in management at Northwestern University, argues, the cover is a "classic example of how indicative posture can be in determining whether people act as though they are in charge. . . . When hierarchical role and physical posture diverge like this, posture seems to be more important in determining how people act and think." No matter their actual titles—in this drawing, at least, Cheney reigns supreme. He rules the roost. He looks like the commander in chief, while the put-upon Bush looks like his attendant, his personal (and at this moment frustrated) manservant. (Is there any need to point out that gender is also at play here, that George, duster at the ready, has been feminized and thus stripped of his power? That Dick has that always reliable sign of masculinity by his side, a stack of beer cans, one of which has been crushed for good measure?)

* * *

Stoop labor. In a midsixties picture by documentary photographer Harvey Richards, six workers are in an open field, the ground furrowed in rows beneath them. Each has his own row. There is no sky, no horizon. The men bend forward at the waist, their backs parallel to the ground. They hold short-handled hoes, midair, midswing. All wear brimmed hats to protect against the sun. They are most likely cultivating lettuce, peppers, strawberries, or sugar beets. Likely, too, they are *braceros* (farmhands, from the Spanish *brazo*, "arm"), Mexican citizens brought to the United States on short-term labor contracts. In 1961, the standard contract paid fifty cents an hour plus a daily food allowance of $1.15. Upon arrival, the workers were taken to processing centers and fumigated with DDT.

There is one other figure in the picture. The crew chief. He oversees all the workers, all the rows. His back is to the camera. Dark jacket, dark pants. His hands appear to be empty. He is hatless and standing upright.

The stooped worker, the upright boss. (The real boss, the grower, isn't in the picture; in another photo by Richards he's sailing his yacht.) The short-handled hoe, *el cortito*, "the short one," was a tool originally brought to the Unites States in the late nineteenth century, probably by Japanese agricultural laborers. Growers later mandated its use because, with a handle of eighteen inches, it required that the farmworker remain in a crouched position while working. Some growers claimed that Mexicans were particularly well suited to the short-handled hoe because of their short stature and low center of gravity. A spokesperson for the beet growers' association, while acknowledging that stoop labor was degrading, said that no white men "reared and educated in our schools . . . [should] have . . . to bend their backs and skin their fingers to pull those little beets. . . . Let us have the only class of labor that will do the work." Economics, class, race, social status: *el cortito*, in a physical way, made manifest the prevailing societal order. "By forcing [the workers] to stoop over," said Peter Liebhold, curator at the National Museum of American History, "it showed who was really in control."

It also, potentially, condemned the farmhand as a slouch. "With the long-handled hoe I can't tell whether they are working or just leaning on their hoes," one supervisor said. "With the short-handled hoe, I know when they are not working by how often they stand up." It was a simple logic; *el cortito* as a means of surveillance. Crouching meant working; standing meant slacking off. And standing could get a worker fired (a twist on the policy at Vassar, where slouching could get a student kicked out; both situations, however, ruled by Darwinian dynamics, equate erect posture with power). Standing meant less lettuce, fewer beets, fewer rows, less profit. A standing worker was unproductive; there were plenty more across the border where he or she came from.

In 1973, farmworkers in California's Salinas Valley, fed up with the degradations of stoop labor, doused their short-handled hoes with gasoline and set them on fire. In 1975, the state banned the use of the short-handled hoe, based on medical testimony about its hazards ("tissue injury," "limitation of motion," "severe back pain," "degeneration of the intervertebral discs," "complete physical disability"). "I walked . . . bent forward like a gorilla," one farmworker said. But growers' efforts to resurrect *el cortito* persisted. Several years later, former farmworker Jessie De La Cruz challenged state officials: "Stand up and hold the tips of your shoes and walk up and down this room and see how many times you can do it."

* * *

In 2003, at the start of the Iraq War, I went to Oaxaca for a month. As I walked down Andador Macedonio Alcalá, the pedestrian street running through the city center, I encountered women who sat on the sidewalk asking for money. Sometimes they were alone, sometimes with a child. The child, often a boy, was the front man, the PR guy, the one who engaged with the public. Maybe he played the guitar, or carved a bear. The woman was the good cop, mute, immobile, suffering in silence; the boy the bad one (but not too bad, because that would be self-defeating), pesky, nagging, resentful, sad, but often a charmer. That was part of the pitch, the plea. How could you resist him? Sometimes he had a knowing and sullen awareness that made you feel exposed, that suggested he knew what you were up to, what you both were up to, and at the very least he would not let it go unacknowledged. Woman and child worked in tandem. They worked to pull on your heartstrings. (A 2002 study on almsgiving in Moscow and Prague examining various motivators for giving, such as religious reasons and social justice concerns, cited empathy as the primary motivator and noted that one of the triggers for empathy is the childlike appearance of the person[s] in need.) At first I didn't give any money. I walked past without stopping. If you were generous you could say I was overwhelmed. If you were cynical you could say my middle-class comforts were being eroded. I myself harbored both of these views, self-pity and resentment. Then, back in my room, which for six hundred dollars a month included blue-and-yellow Mexican tiles in the kitchen area, biweekly cleaning, and a five-gallon starter jug of bottled water, I felt ashamed of myself. Okay, I would give; of course I would give. I would give X dollars per day until it ran out. That would be my strategy. But propped in bed, with a mosquito circling my head, I couldn't rid my mind of the possibility I was being scammed. I remembered the time I backed my parents' car into someone else's and left a note with my phone number on the damaged vehicle. I was sure I had done the right thing, my response an outcome of my entire upbringing; but when I got home and told my parents, my father, rather than saluting my conduct, condemned it. Why did I leave a phone number? Our insurance rates would go up. How could I be so naïve? Stupid was what he implied. It's a dog-eat-dog world, he said, knowingly, bitterly, in an effort to educate me and yet at the same time, as if I weren't there, confirming for himself the whole wretched state of affairs. And no way was he going to be the sap left behind.

* * *

Why do beggars sit on the ground? Why do they lie at the feet of others? Are the women I saw in Oaxaca assuming a scripted role in the fraught choreography between supplicant and supplicated? *Ptochos*, the Greek word for "beggar," literally means a person who crouches or cringes and is closely linked to *ptox*, or hare, described by Homer in the *Iliad* as a "cowering creature." Since the ancient Greeks, sitting has been the posture of supplication and part of its very etymology. A fifteenth-century fresco in the Vatican's Chapel of Nicholas V shows Saint Lawrence bestowing alms on a seated beggar. Lawrence, reflecting the wealth of the church, is dressed in a tasseled and brocaded vestment and looms over the crouching petitioner with his crutch and sackcloth. Rembrandt's famous etchings of beggars depict them, whether seated or standing, in hunched, doleful postures.

Beggars, of course, are not the only supplicants who sit, crouch, or prostrate. In ancient Greece, downed soldiers tossed away their weapons, approached the victors with empty, outstretched hands, and knelt in supplication, hoping to have their lives spared. Social inferiors such as slaves and brides appealed for entry into their new homes through a ritual that included sitting by the hearth. Mourners, in a profound demonstration of grief, abased themselves by spreading manure or ashes on their bodies and rolling on the ground. In medieval Germany, one Marsilius the cartwright, stricken with lumbago as a punishment for blasphemy, climbed up to the shrine of Saint Anno bent to the ground like "a piece of cattle," seeking to be healed. Jews have their *davening*, Catholics their genuflection, Buddhists their *raihai* (lying on the ground and lifting the hands, a gesture meant to suggest raising the Buddha's feet above one's head), Muslims their five daily prostrations.

* * *

In the end, I reached into my stash of coins and meted them out. There was no discernible logic to my decision-making. I gave in an attempt to be left alone. I gave dutifully, as if guilt, not money, were the currency of this transaction and I could hand it off for a sentiment more worthy. I gave grudgingly, which, according to Maimonides' celebrated Eight Degrees of Charity, is the least meritorious. After a month, after I visited the Ethnobotanical Garden, the Santo Domingo de Guzmán Church, decorated with over sixty thousand sheets of gold leaf, the Museo de Arte Contemporáneo, the ruins at Monte Albán, the rug vendors of Santa María del Tule; after I sampled several but not all seven kinds of mole, tried *tejate*, a drink made with corn, cacao, and mamey fruit, which I could barely swallow, and *nieve de tuna*, prickly pear sorbet, which I loved; after I marched against the Iraq War and attended the Good Friday processional, where penitents in purple robes and conical hats looked disturbingly like Ku Klux Klansmen; after I bought four blue-and-white ceramic bowls, a set of miniature carved musicians, an exuberantly macabre *calavera*, or skull, and Mayordomo chocolate at the market; after I bought an extra suitcase for my purchases, I went home.

* * *

No, *Kaicho* said. Again. I had to bow again. His face was stern with displeasure. I was bowing incorrectly. Do again. This went on a number of times, the Japanese master, the American student, the improper bowing, which, with each attempt, became stiffer, more tentative and confused. We were at *honbu*, the New York headquarters for the World Seido Karate Organization, and this was my test for second-degree black belt. There was an audience for my debacle: my teachers were watching, as well as *Kaicho*'s senior students, and the other black belt candidates too, eager supplicants, hoping to pass on to the next rank. I had spoken a few words about myself, my martial arts training—one of the test requirements, in the Japanese tradition of public speaking—and then, at the end of my presentation, as custom and etiquette dictated, I'd faced *Kaicho* and bowed.

That's how we begin and end all exchanges on the *dojo* floor, with a show of mutual courtesies. It's a way to give and receive respect, and to indicate the sincerity of our intent. Only now I was bowing, not to my practice partner, or my teachers, but to my teachers' teacher, the master himself, a ninth-degree black belt and world-renowned figure in the martial arts.

No.

I don't remember if *Kaicho* told me what was wrong with my bow, or my teachers did, or one of the other students, but eventually I understood the offense came down to my arms, which, when I bowed, flew out from my body, toward *Kaicho*, in a movement that could be construed as aggressive and disrespectful. I did not display the proper "bodily attitude." Instead of expressing respect and deference, I'd inadvertently conveyed an insult.

My teachers and I went to lunch. My perceived transgression lay heavily on me. If I had not bowed properly before, I felt bowed now, weighed down by my mistake and the concurrent public flaying. My teachers were unsettled too. They'd wanted me to shine in New York, and already I'd foundered. My failure, if only a little, rubbed off on them. The mood was grim. There, in a Greek diner in Chelsea, waiting for my lunch, I practiced bowing in an aisle next to our table. My teachers offered tips, castigations, amendments. Ever the good student, I concentrated on keeping my wayward arms by my sides, on reigning them in so as not to offend until, finally, my desire to do well by my teachers and do well on the test was surpassed by my growing sense of discomfort and my awareness of the spectacle this had become—a white middle-aged American woman bowing repeatedly in a New York City lunch spot while the server skirted her—and so, in an effort to preserve my self-respect and bring this scene to an end, I refused my teachers' entreaties to bow one more time, and sat down to my Greek salad instead.

* * *

A year into his first term, Barack Obama and his bowing troubles were all over the news. Obama, on a 2009 trip to Japan, greeted Emperor Akihito—the son of Hirohito, the media was quick to remind us, followed by references to Pearl Harbor and the Axis powers—with a nearly ninety-degree bow, which was seen by former vice president Dick Cheney and others as groveling. Said Cheney, "There is no reason for an American president to bow to anyone. Our friends and allies don't expect it and our enemies see it as a sign of weakness." "How Low Will He Go?" echoed a headline in the *Los Angeles Times*. Conservative blogger Michelle Malkin went so far as to call the president a "water boy," cringingly reminiscent of the word *boy* as once used for black males. Even those who saw Obama's bow as culturally sensitive noted that he simultaneously shook hands with Emperor Akihito, a gesture both "jarring and inappropriate." The Japanese media, for its part, remained discreetly silent about Obama's bow, but bloggers throughout the country voiced their approval: "What a bow!" "Obama's huge!" "He's really trying hard to meet the Japanese way." One respondent mused thoughtfully, "The emperor or the Pope, the President or the Prime Minister, whoever is greater is not something that . . . can be decided objectively." And then there's Tokyo-based journalist Andrew Horvat, who in his book *Japanese beyond Words* (2000) offers an even more telling take on the Anglo world's discomfort with bowing when he recalls that after living in Japan for many years, he returned home to the West for a visit and inadvertently bowed upon entering his boss's office. "Don't bow," his boss said. "Don't you know white men don't bow!" Did this sentiment possibly underlie Dick Cheney's criticism of Barack Obama? As long as Obama, our first African-American president, was playing a white man's game, he should abide by a white man's rules?

Did the president go too far? In a society where road construction signs show a man bowing to drivers as an apology for any inconvenience, what are the rules? In Japan people bow to apologize, make a request, offer gifts, sympathy, or condolences; it's a gesture of greeting, respect, deference, thanks; go into a department store, and you're likely to be welcomed by a bowing greeter; take a train, and the conductor bows on her way out of the car. Some anthropologists suggest that bowing may be hard-wired into Japanese infants, who traditionally have been strapped onto their mothers' backs: when the mothers bow, the babies do too.

Bowing is an expression of Japan's complex social hierarchy. Here turn-of-the century American educator and scholar Alice Mabel Bacon, who taught at the Gakushūin School in Tokyo for a year (alumni include Emperor Akihito, writer Yukio Mishima, and Yoko Ono), describes her experience in a September 20, 1888, letter home to her family:

> When the bell rings I go to my recitation room and there, ranged in line outside of the door, is my class awaiting me. I bow as low as I can, the pupils bow still lower, and then go into the room. They take their places quietly and stand; I bow from my place

> at the teacher's desk, again the girls bow, and take their seats, and for fifty minutes we labor with the intricacies of the English language. The signal for the close of the lesson is given by a man who walks through the corridors clapping a pair of wooden clappers. When I hear that sound, I finish the lesson, and bow to the class, who all bow, rise, marching quietly out of the door range themselves in order and wait for me. I walk out, bow to them once more, they make a farewell obeisance, and quietly disperse.

Note that in the course of fifty minutes, teacher and students exchange bows four times. Note too that when they bow, the students, in recognition of Bacon's position as instructor, make sure to go lower than she does.

According to *Tofugu*, a self-described "wonky Japanese language and culture blog," there are five levels of bowing in Japan. The first is the nod-bow, which is not really a bow but a slight tilt of the head. It's the most casual, reserved for good friends. It's also used by a high-ranking person as a form of acknowledgment—boss to worker, for instance. Next is the greeting bow, called *eshaku*, a fifteen-degree bend from the waist used between people who either know each other (but are not intimates) or are equals. The respect bow, *keirei*, is thirty degrees. It's meant for one's employer or people who are higher ranking on the social scale. What *Tofugu* calls the "highest respect bow," *saikeirei*, is forty-five degrees. "Say you screw up, big time . . . perhaps you made some cars that accelerate to 80mph and crash into things and you need to apologize . . ." This bow expresses respect, and apology and/or regret as well. The last bow is the kneeling bow, head to the floor. You don't see it very often, says *Tofugu*. Generally it's reserved for the martial arts (in Seido karate, we perform a series of seated bows to begin and end each class: to the *shinzen*, the ceremonial center of the *dojo*; *Kaicho*, the founder; the instructors in order of rank; and the senior students). Or for highly egregious behavior. In 1996, six corporate executives, implicated in a scandal in which thousands of hemophiliacs contracted HIV from contaminated blood products, dropped to their knees and lowered their foreheads to the floor in a public show of profound apology.

As for the proper way to bow, start with the feet together. Bend slowly; you don't want to look like a duck bobbing frantically for something to eat, cautions *How to Be Polite in Japanese*, a primer used by my friend B. when she went to live in Japan. Men bow with hands at their sides, women with hands folded in front of them. Eyes are averted.

* * *

Does the debutante turn into the dowager, the dowager with her dowager's hump?

Is that what I've become? I see an elderly woman with a rounded back walking down the street, and wonder if I'm looking at myself. The girl has a slouch, the woman has a hump. The dowager's hump started making the news in the late 1920s. It was "unbeautiful," unstylish ("a too fat back, a billowing dowager's hump. . . . Nothing can destroy chic like structural defects," claimed an article in the *Chicago Daily Tribune*), a sign of female dotage. Or, as a columnist for the *Boston Globe* wrote, "The dowager's hump is a placard of slowed up brain action." My friend J. had a spinal fusion several years ago, and although she unequivocally considers the surgery a success because it alleviated her debilitating pain, I can't cast aside my lingering skepticism because it left her looking old and stooped over. Is that the source of our fear and ridicule of the dowager? That inch by inch she's making her way back to earth? Closer to the ground and closer to death? (In fact, a recent study by the UCLA School of Medicine cited hyperkyphosis, or dowager's hump, as a risk factor for early death.) Or does my fear stem from concerns not quite so weighty? Is it simply based on good old-fashioned vanity? Not long ago I was talking to a robust woman nearing eighty, and with no small hint of smugness we joked about the follies of youth. You look twenty yourself, she said, and in spite of my offhand dismissiveness and the utter improbability of her remark, I took a measure of pride and comfort in it. She must not have been looking at my dowager's hump.

And who is this dowager? With her connotations of dowdiness, desiccation, and dotage. In common usage of the word, she's an elderly woman who hints at money and stodginess. Often she's portrayed as a matron with an arch sense of dignity. By definition, she is someone whose luster is borrowed. She serves in her spouse's stead, though she may in fact have no real authority. (There are notable exceptions. Take the nineteenth-century Empress Dowager Cixi, for instance, who started out as a concubine and ended up ruling China for forty-seven years. Or Liliana Dahlgren, the Dowager Duchess of Medina Sidonia, who in a 2008 deathbed ceremony wed her dying lover, Spanish aristocrat Luisa Isabel Álvarez de Toledo, Twenty-First Duchess of Medina Sidonia, and took over Europe's largest private archive, housing medieval documents dating from the thirteenth century.) The dowager-princess, dowager-queen, dowager-duchess, dowager-empress, dowager-lady. Would we ever have called Jackie Kennedy the dowager-First Lady? The tradition doesn't hold in this country, where our aristocracy is based on money and class rather than royalty; where we often use the word *dowager* as an insult for the female elderly. (In an ambiguous reversal of this tendency, writer-comic Julie Klausner urges women to stop acting like "pubeless, twee, Anime-eyed" girls and start being age appropriate. "You can make your own modern womanhood—there's no need to fear the dowager.") Kennedy was, however, a debutante of the first order, named debutante of the year for the 1947–48 season. What's more, Kennedy, who never seemed to age (until she died of lymphoma, precipitously and startlingly, in 1994), was a model of perfect posture. As First Lady, she received letters from women all over the country remarking on her "regal bearing." "You are a queen," one woman wrote. "My daughter wants to be like you." For her part, Kennedy attributed her posture to years of equestrian training.

* * *

Right now I am slouching. I'm sitting in my Herman Miller Aeron chair, which, being expensive and ergonomically sound, is supposed to aid in good posture, but neither the chair nor its occupant is succeeding. I've succumbed to old habits. There is no posture cop to wag a finger or slap me with a fine. I am unobserved. Nor am I wearing the Sitting Pose Corrector and Reminder Alarm, a red, bird-shaped electronic gadget with internal sensors that detect slumping posture and emit, presumably, chirping sounds to wake the wearer and warn her of her transgression. Made in Japan and put out by DealExtreme, it goes for $8.43. Officially tagged with a diagnosis of osteoporosis almost ten years ago, I'm like my friend J., getting shorter. A new acquaintance recently distinguished me from my partner by designating me "the little one." I've lost a few inches; how many more to go?

In the meantime, I turn back to another era, when posture queens all over the country donned their crowns. They won scholarships, new mattresses, TV sets, and trophies. Miss Perfect Spine, Miss Perfect Back, Miss Good Posture. "Cheesecake," *Time* magazine said. "Michigan chiropractors dutifully pored over dozens of candidates' X rays to find the girl with the best intervertebral fibrocartilages." But along with the familiar elements of prurience and prudery—the hallmarks of beauty contests ever since Barnum and Bailey tried to launch one in the mid-nineteenth century—there's outright oddness too. In one picture from the 1957 national contest, three contestants in evening gowns and earrings rest their elbows on light boxes displaying lit x-rays of their heads and torsos. From the chest up they are permed hairdos, penciled eyebrows, glossy smiles; below they are bony illuminations. Their vertebrae look like dice neatly stacked. Part kewpie, part skeleton, the women could be mistaken for a circus act or subjects in a Cindy Sherman photograph. I probe the x-rays like the x-rays probe them. Rib cage, pelvis, femur. On one, empty white disks of earrings hang suspended from a skull; the jaw sits partially open. On another, shoulder sockets jut like machine parts. Whose dream is this? What do these x-rays reveal? What goes undetected? Who imagined we could really learn anything about these women from their ghostly portraits?

The Knife

In my martial arts training I'm learning to use the knife. *The* is the operative word here: *the* knife. The definite article, underscoring the definitive nature of the thing itself. That's how we talk in my *dojo*: the knife, the *bo*, the *jo*, the *sai*. All the weapons made preeminent by language: no indefinite *a* for any of them. But the knife, well, the knife is in a category of its own. *Bo* and *jo*—the long and short stick, respectively—and *sai*—a three-pronged, trident-like instrument—have their origins in agriculture; at least that's one version of martial arts history. Originally tools used by Okinawan farmers—the *bo*, for instance, a pole for carrying water, the *sai* a dibber for making holes in the ground for seeds—they were secretly transformed into weapons to oppose the conquering Japanese. The domestic made lethal—that's the legend. The knife, however, is, and always has been, an instrument of cutting. On the *dojo* floor I hold it in my hand.

I buy into the myth. Nobody employs the *bo* or the *sai* as a weapon today. They belong to another time, another era—I can learn their use guilt-free. I am merely delving into history. Of course, I can see that a *bo* and a baseball bat may have similar martial application. A baseball bat, benign against a ball, is crushing against a skull.

Homeowners hide them under their beds. And baseball itself, the sport I have long loved, acknowledges the bat's potential in a funny kind of way. Why was Frank Thomas, former designated hitter for the White Sox, nicknamed the Big Hurt? Because when he hit the ball out of the park, he crushed it. The ball, it might be said, making its way across the sky, sees stars. In black belt class, we practice an overhead *bo* strike to the top of the head and another, diagonal, strike to the temple. Sometimes we say that the arc of the *bo* is similar to that of a baseball bat. I've heard myself say that. I picture the bat slicing through the air, the bat I held in my own hands once, on summer nights when my father tossed a sixteen-inch softball over the makeshift plate, and the stars, emerging one by one, dotted the sky overhead; and the point at which, in my mind, the bat makes contact and the ball flies off—that's the point where I focus my *bo* strike to the temple.

But a woman who carries a knife? That gives me pause. Unlike the *bo*, the knife is not a relic. Its function has not been consigned to history, although, in an impulse both romantic and distancing, I do remember seeing *West Side Story* when I was ten, the Jets squaring off against the Sharks, each wielding knives. My mother took me to see that film. I learned the words to "I Feel Pretty." Like Maria, I primped in front of a mirror. And though, at the end, Maria was reputedly killed by a rival gang member, and Tony, upon learning of her supposed death, inconsolably begs for the same, it is not lost love or feuding factions that are forever fixed in my mind but the Rumble, thrilling, threatening, nimble, acrobatic, accompanied by the chill glint of blades.

* * *

Years later, at nineteen, I went into a downtown sporting goods store for a backpack and a knife. I was going to Costa Rica; the backpack—army-green vintage, brown leather straps—was for jeans, D. H. Lawrence's *Lady Chatterley's Lover*, a six-month supply of sanitary napkins because I was worried I wouldn't be able to get them so close to the equator. The knife would fit into a side pocket. Be independent, my mother used to tell me. She meant: *Don't worry about what other people say, listen to me.* Even if I wasn't sure how to be independent, I knew how to shop. Knife, pack, map, stamps, flashlight, mosquito repellent: I'd be ready for anything.

It was hard to buy a Swiss Army knife; there were so many lined up under the counter, with so many attachments. Did I need a corkscrew? But I hardly drank. A nail file? A pair of those tiny, baby scissors? The knives were beautiful, a dark glossy red, stamped with the signature silver cross. The blades fit snugly inside the handle, each incised with a moonlike notch curved to fit your fingernail. Some of the blades, jaunty with precision, were already pulled out, at the ready. I was hesitant, confused. The salesman waited silently on the other side of the counter. Suddenly, his silence felt like all the reasons I might need a knife to begin with: as a counter against fear and contempt and scorn and judgment and accusation; something I could put between myself and the world, the world's perceptions of me, and my perceptions of myself. Finally, I chose a streamlined one, with a can opener. It had a teepee-like tent and the word *CAMPING* etched in silver. I'd never been camping before. The closest I'd come was sleeping next to an open window.

In Costa Rica, I carried the knife with me over the mountains. *Leave me alone*, I learned to say. I practiced under my breath. *Déjame en paz.* But when the police picked me up at two o'clock in the morning—an American woman walking alone on the Inter-American Highway—I had no words to explain to myself or them what I was doing. It's my birthday, it's my birthday, I kept repeating in my truncated Spanish, as if that would account for why, four hours earlier, driving back to San José with friends, I'd decided to walk and gotten out of the car, buttressed only by a cautionary phrase and the Swiss Army knife in my pocket.

The police held me for several hours. In a nearby town a man had been found dead, and I was, after all, suspicious. I sat in the backseat of their car while they alternately asked questions and ignored me. They talked among themselves in rapid-fire Spanish made more isolating by the frightening circumstances. At one point someone offered me a glass of water and a banana, and although I'd been told to drink only bottled water in Costa Rica, I accepted gratefully. Waiting for my innocence to become apparent, or at least my foolishness—it's my birthday, it's my birthday—I felt the weight of the knife sitting in my pocket; I had a weapon, a concealed weapon, on my person, and while I hadn't used it, or used it only as a prop, a lucky charm, the dead man wasn't so lucky. Would I be searched? The knife discovered? Night turned into day, and in the light of dawn the police revealed that the man had not been killed—he had taken his own life, a *suicida*, and though we did not have a shared language to express our subdued relief that life's burdens had not overtaken one of us that night, we fell into a close and oddly comforting silence on the drive back to San José, until one of the policemen turned to me and said, with avuncular consternation, Do not do such a thing again.

* * *

I started my martial arts training the day the Gulf War began. Driving to the *dojo* for my first class, I listened while public radio broadcast the first accounts of American fighter-bombers raiding Iraq. It was early evening in Chicago, and already dark; early morning and still dark in Baghdad. The city shook from the force of the explosions, one reporter said. I parked the car, upped the heat; the sky was like a fireworks finale on the Fourth of July, the report continued. I felt afraid, imagining the low flight of planes over *my* neighborhood. Would I be safe in the basement? Then I felt ashamed for hoping the war would stay *over there*; for hoping I could oppose it from a safe distance. We've just bombed Iraq, I said to the person at the front desk, compelled to tell someone a war had started.

During the next few weeks, as the war continued, I learned how to make a fist. Scud missiles landed on Tel Aviv. Turkish soldiers threw frozen chickens at the Kurds, striking many in the head. I'd used my fists one time before, punching a pillow so hard I bloodied knuckles on both hands. You are defeating your weakness, the long-haired Gestalt therapist pronounced, as others in the group looked on. I never went back. Now I had other teachers. This is your weapon, they said, the first two knuckles at the base of your fingers, the knuckles of your index and middle fingers. This is what will strike your target. On the *dojo* floor, a polished wood surface overhung with Japanese curtains called *norens*, the body became a battlefield. Targets: solar plexus, floating rib, temple. Weapons: back fist, hammer fist, sword peak, knife foot. We did pushups on our knuckles to toughen them. What did it mean—if anything—to study a martial art when American military personnel referred to Iraqi civilian casualties as collateral damage? Do not be glib, I told myself. Do not look for easy metaphors. *Kiai*, the instructors said, and on the last punch we yelled—not unlike a war cry—together. The sound was exhilarating.

* * *

In 1982, Ann and I were robbed. We lived in the first-floor apartment of a three-flat. Ann came home first, four-thirty in the afternoon, the front door slightly ajar. It was stupid, she says. She says that now, but then she walked right in. They had taken the usual stuff—stereo, jewelry; it's what they left I remember. Our underpants tossed across the bedroom floor; a knife sitting on Ann's antique walnut dresser. It was our knife, from our kitchen; what I think of as a butcher knife. The robbers had, obviously, carried it around with them, and when they were done, dropped it on the dresser.

Ann is a cook. By profession she's a graphic designer. She likes tools. She's proficient with a compass and an X-Acto knife. She likes to strip woodwork, cane chairs. On our first date she served me rabbit stew, sort of like beef stroganoff. It's French, she told me. The knife on the dresser was hers, a Sabatier; French too. Large, heavy, with a polished black handle. Sabatier is a family name, famous French knife makers, cream of the crop.

The police dusted the knife for prints, but when they were done with it we put it back in the kitchen. They never caught the guys or found our stuff, though later we did get some money from the insurance. We called our friends to tell them we'd been robbed. Other than that, we wrote down the serial numbers of electronic and other equipment, and put the numbers in an accordion folder labeled *Important Papers*. We went on. We cooked a lot in those days. It was part of our early romance. Russian vegetable tart, popovers, Finnish rusks, croissants, calzones, polenta pizza, *zuppa inglese*. We grated, peeled, minced, chopped.

In the years since then, we've let our knives grow dull. I don't think it's too harsh to say that, inadvertently, we've abused them. Like life in general, I guess, with equal measures of neglect, despair, surprise, wonder. Once my great-aunt, then ninety-four, said she wanted to buy us something. What do you need? We went into Bloomingdale's, the housewares department. She hung heavily on my elbow. Get what you need, she repeated. The salesman, a handsome guy with a name tag that said Carlo, talked about all the knives, Wüsthof-Trident, J. A. Henckels, Sabatier, KitchenAid. Some were factory stamped—and here he took a tone of offhand dismissal—others—nodding in approval—hand-forged, high-carbon stainless steel. He spoke with enthusiasm and knowledge. Which one do you recommend? We sell a lot of these as wedding presents, he pointed. My aunt threw him her winning, blue-eyed smile. Sabatier, I said, the basic set: chef, bread, boning, slicer, parer. Get the sharpener too, my aunt insisted.

* * *

Some people like their knives dull. They feel safer. My friend M. is that way. She prefers kitchen knives with no bite, no grip; she'll hack away, no matter. Recently, however, she moved to a new city, a new job, and, perhaps in celebration of the fact that she was not required, for the time being, to live a life of vigilant downscaling, bought a new set of knives.

But having bought them, she was afraid. Arrayed on her kitchen counter, they were a hazard. A threat. She moved the knives to an inconvenient corner of the kitchen, a place where she would not have ready access; where she would have to pick one up with deliberation, not impulse. She would break these knives in, but slowly; she would wait for them to become blunt and reassuring.

She told me this over lunch at a café. Her dark eyes had an expression both wry and wounded. When she wasn't looking, I'd noticed how thin her legs were, how she ate her Caesar salad cautiously, almost leaf by leaf, chewing slowly, as if she couldn't quite afford the pleasure of gusto. Dimly, I remembered how years before on a drizzly London street, she'd asked me if I ever felt like giving up, like I couldn't go on. We'd just passed a wall covered with graffiti, Dance to the Death slashed across it. I hadn't felt that way, but I didn't feel immune either. I sensed that her despair could be mine, momentarily. Now, in the café, I thought I knew what M. was afraid of. Once you have a tool, you're likely to use it. One swipe of the wrist, or two if you want to be sure, that's all it would take. Better to keep the knife at arm's length.

* * *

Let me say something about the knives in my *dojo*: they're fake. We call them practice knives. Rubber or wood, the blade edge is decidedly dull. The pliant rubber one—I saw a similar version in a toy store, complete with cape and mask—reminds me of Halloween. The wooden knife, smooth, polished, heavy, grained, is beautiful, in its way. We have a weapons wall in our *dojo* where the practice weapons, in an expression of sincerity, are mounted and displayed. There are two other knives, not displayed, with tooled-leather sheaths and ornate handles, that a student brought back from Africa as gifts. One of the handles is a carving of a woman with a scarified face. Once, feeling the grooves on the woman's cheeks, I wondered how these cuts were made. With a knife such as this? I ran my finger along the blade, unsharpened, and realized, with a start, that for a second I'd been lulled into thinking this was a real woman, real flesh. Real knives, we keep these hidden away in the *shinzen*, our *dojo* altar.

Karate means "empty hand." First we learn to kick and punch, block and parry, and only after several years of empty-handed practice do we pick up the knife. It's an earned responsibility. Whenever one of our teachers says Go get a knife, a jaunty nervousness fills the *dojo*. The knife is the weapon of our nightmares. It is our oldest weapon. One night Ann dreamt that she was slashed across the back, all the way from her hip to her shoulder. She felt an enormous rush of air, and woke up cold and trembling.

We wield the knife in order to learn how to defend against it. To be good defenders we must be good attackers.

I'd never wielded a knife before. I wasn't the kind of kid who hid behind a mountain of dirt waiting to vanquish my opponent. I dressed up as a lady on Halloween. Ann played those games; she was that kid. There's a picture of her, four or five years old, skinny as now, with long braids, straight bangs, overalls, a holster at her hips, six-shooters drawn and ready. The expression on her face is one of impish determination. I sat on the couch one night after a karate class, holding a table knife in my hand. The knife was from the set of flatware I inherited after my father died, but my mother was the one, a long time before, who'd selected it, and I thought of it as somehow reflecting her, stylish and classy. Plain, with a little scrolly flourish on the handle, a matte silver finish, engraved with *International Stainless Deluxe* on the back. I looked at the knife. I felt foolish. I gripped it, not like I was going to cut a piece of chicken or asparagus, but in simulation of a stab. I cried a little, just enough, even though I was alone, to feel embarrassed. Attack with a knife? How was I supposed to know how to do this?

We are very ceremonial with our knives. We are polite attackers. We have rituals of engagement. We bow, display our knives openly so as to harbor no secrets, assume a fighter's stance. I love the bow, I appreciate that moment when I hold the knife, blade down and away from my body, in my extended right hand, the left over my heart, and I meet the eyes of my partner, who, earnest and empty-handed, bows back. There is a moment before attack.

And then? And then, we're down to business. We learn the language, and mechanics, of attack.

There are grips. Regular grip, blade above the fist; reverse, blade below. Palm to palm, grip to grip. And strikes. Slash, stab. Horizontal, diagonal, left to right, right to left. Over the top, like Norman Bates in *Psycho*. Our teacher makes a rueful laugh. A knife strike, in order to be maximally effective, must be delivered with the whole body. Like this. Penetrate their space. Use the hip. It is a wild and awkward choreography, pairs of wide-eyed students skirting the room, yet even the most inexpert among us occasionally lands a hit.

I feel the knife as it lands, reverberating back in my hand.

Of course, there's defense as well. That's the point, isn't it. Evade, hollow, redirect, disarm. Finish with a disabling blow. We guard with the fleshy undersides of our forearms turned away from the attacker to protect the veins from being slashed.

At the end we bow again.

* * *

I take an informal survey. I have a sample of two. What does it mean to fight like a girl? To be uncommitted, S. says. To fight like a man means you're not really trying to hit the face; you're trying to hit the back of the head. To fight like a girl means you bounce off. You're cringing. Demonstrating, S. throws a wayward punch, her thumb stuck on the inside, and I resist the urge to correct it.

Ann, a martial artist herself, says to fight like a girl means not even fighting. Hitting with the bottom of the fists, she adds, hair pulling, scratching.

B., who's not part of my survey but knows about hair pulling and was, in high school, a greaser from Cicero—the Chicago suburb that wouldn't let Martin Luther King Jr. march down its streets—once told me that some of the toughest girls in school ruffed their hair and then stuck in razor blades so that if anyone tried to grab it they got a handful.

For my part, I slapped my brother across the face when I was four and he was a baby. On Sunday mornings, our parents still sleeping, I waited for him to pull himself up by the bars of the crib, his blond head peeking over the top, and then I crawled out of bed in the room we now had to share and slapped him until he stared crying, and my father, in his boxer shorts and undershirt, groggily came to console him. When my father left the room, I hit him again.

Years later, I resorted to a weapon. Angry for a reason I no longer remember, I dug my braces—a blade of sorts and what I had available—into my brother's forehead, previously unmarked and smooth and pink as porcelain, and hovering over him, both of us splayed atop my parents' bed, I waited for the skin to pull apart, the parallel cuts, small and precise, to widen, the blood to bloom and bead up, the terror, on his face and probably on mine, to spread.

Does my brother have a scar? I'm not sure. His forehead is high, and his hair, still blond, is receding.

As we walked through Indian Boundary Park one night, a neighbor with half an index finger, a stub I stared at, started counting. He was twenty, I was sixteen. Overhead, the trees interlaced their limbs. The sound of our footsteps seemed to follow us. After each number he paused, a gap. I tried to stay a step ahead. My mother played mahjongg with his. *One bam, two crak.* Even now, I can hear them making their bids.

At *three* his hand, the one with the foreshortened finger, landed on my shoulder.

He grinned.

Now there's a self-defense poster in the *dojo* locker room. I look at it while I'm getting dressed. "Learn How to Fight like a Girl," it says, with a picture of a woman, palm heel extended, warding off her attacker. I catch a look at myself in the mirror. My belly, which should be taut from sit-ups—we do them regularly in class—is, instead, like a slab of clay stuck with thumbprints, making me look soft and doughy. Cellulite, and I feel embarrassed, not so much for having it but for having become, without acceding to it, a cliché. Shaking my head, I turn back to the poster. *Learn how to fight like a girl.* Another cliché, but stood on end. Once I took a self-defense class during a time beset by self-doubt and confusion, when I lived in a faded green apartment above an elderly Italian woman who complained that my footsteps were too loud. Once a week for six weeks I aimed my newly formed front kick at an imaginary attacker's knee, while at home I padded softly across my living room floor. At the end of the class I was awarded a certificate, and several months later, carting boxes down the stairs, I moved out.

* * *

Ann and I need another paring knife.

This time I go, not to Bloomingdale's, but to Chef's Catalog—overpriced, my aunt says, but she's too frail to come with me, and besides I'm a sucker. It's the store for the home chef. When I ask for Sabatier, the saleswoman—late twenties, robust, authoritative, a professional, she tells me—says they don't carry that line anymore. Seems that somewhere along the way, the company sold its name to anyone who would buy it, and it was all downhill from there.

She shakes her head with regret but perks up pronto and leads me to the Wüsthof-Trident. They're the best. Before I know it, I've got a paring knife in my hand. Full tang, no-slip grip. She remarks on the perfect balance.

I ask the price, but it's a diversion. How can I tell her I don't want to buy a German knife? I'm uneasy about German products. When I was a kid, our next-door neighbors were German, and I didn't think anything of it until their dog started barking incessantly across the fence. My father talked to the neighbor—by trade a baker who brought home stacks of confections in cardboard boxes—but the dog didn't let up. The Germans have never liked us, my father said, his voice suggesting that this was the final and determining remark in a long, tiresome conversation; by *us* he meant Jews. I practically rolled my eyes, because history was the past and I was a modern, optimistic child, but all these years later, I'm his daughter. In the store, I make an easy connection between cutlery and the Nazis. I'd like to say I already knew about the Night of the Long Knives, also called the Röhm-Putsch, the Great Blood Purge, when Hitler ordered the murder of four hundred Brownshirts, but I only learned about that later. Did Wüsthof-Trident manufacture daggers for the SS? The saleswoman moves on to another knife, the J. A. Henckels, but it's a lost cause. Yes, she says, when I ask if both companies are German, in an underhanded effort, I suppose, to point it out to her. Do I think, once enlightened, she'll come around and disavow the product? And they're located in the same town, a block from each other, she adds, like it's a coincidence, but to me it's a conspiracy.

Shamelessly I go on. Have the companies been around a long time? Since before World War II? I'm trying to re-create the lines of historical culpability, but the saleswoman can't help me. By now her uninformed answers have taken on a bemused, cautious tone—uh-oh, this customer is a little loony—and I decide to drop it, exiting with what I know to be a lie. I'll be back, I say. All our cutlery goes on sale at the end of the month, she informs me.

At home I head straight to the kitchen. Driving back in the car, I'd remembered another knife, one I bought several years ago, cheap, a manufacturer's special. I bought it at Chef's Catalog. We keep the knives in a slanted wooden block on the counter, and there in the slots at the bottom, where they always sit, are two paring knives: the hand-forged, high-carbon, full-tang Sabatier and the other knife, the one with the flimsy blade—nicked, which is why we need a new one—and molded black plastic handle. I pick it up and look at the logo. J. A. Henckels.

I'm not done. At the library I learn that both Wüsthof-Trident and J. A. Henckels are headquartered in Solingen, a steel town in the Ruhr region. I picture Gary, Indiana, only prettier. There are rolling hills and maybe a child or two in lederhosen. The hills are supersaturated with green. Then I come across a book titled *Collecting the Edged Weapons of the Third Reich*. Solingen, the book says, is known as "the city of swords." Most Nazi daggers came from manufacturers located there. I'm smitten by the alliteration—never mind that it's a translation—which strikes me as happily convenient, like Solingen and swords were meant for each other, and what's more, I'm about to discover something. I look at the photographs of bald-headed master craftsmen in aprons holding knives. Is there guilt, remorse, pride of product? The book has a list of manufacturers: Carl Eickhorn; Richard Herder; Ernest, Pack, and Sohn; Wagner & Lange; Alexander Coppel; Robert Klass; Karl Böker; C. Bertram Reinhr. There are even several Jewish-sounding names—Jacobs and Company, Joseph Wolf—but surely this is impossible. Yet there is no mention of Henckels or Wüsthof-Trident among the companies that supplied the Nazis with blades. Listlessly, as if exhausted by my spirited but fruitless efforts to assign blame, I turn a few more pages. Under a photo of blown-up buildings, a caption says that Solingen suffered grave damage from Allied bombing during the war. Alone at the table, I feel rebuked.

* * *

Twice, I've gone under the knife. First a tonsillectomy and later a nose job. Slight changes to my personal topography. I have a pert nose, a nose I have long thought of as mine, although I have wondered if, confronted with my old nose—which my mother had regarded ruefully—acquaintances would still pause upon discovering I'm Jewish. This saddens me a bit, because I want to be recognized. I'd like to have something that gives it away. But then I was sixteen, and sought only favor.

As for the tonsillectomy, well, it doesn't hurt, I told my brother when it was his turn, but I must have known that was a lie.

Still, in the long run, I have been more traumatized by cutting than being cut. I have not, given the opportunities, demonstrated either adequate precision or speed with the knife, and these skills are essential. You're too slow, my mother once said when I was chopping an onion for the meatloaf, and as she grabbed the knife from me, taking my place at the cutting board, I sensed in her an exasperation so deep, so profound, I was helpless. She meant no harm, I tell myself, recalling the swift fury with which she dispatched the onion. Perhaps she only wanted me to be proficient.

In graduate school as an exercise physiology student, I took a human anatomy class, where in a basement lab we dissected cadavers. I could never, quite, make the cut. There are 206 bones in the human body, 22 in the skull alone, and over 600 skeletal muscles. I would look at the body laid out before me—in this case a woman whose pressed lips and bony feet and taut, wrinkled neck suggested a parsimonious old age—and wonder what prompted her to submit to our fumblings. When she signed up, had she imagined spending her final days under such unsure hands? *Cadaver* is from the Latin *cadere*, "to fall, sink, settle down, decline, perish"; to be, at the end, prone on this dissecting table.

* * *

In the *dojo* locker room, where the conversation not uncommonly turns to targets and weapons, a friend is talking to Ann about the *sai*, the arcane weapon Ann's lately taken a shine to. It's your weapon, the friend says with a nod. Ann demurs, but I know that she's pleased.

Do *I* have a weapon?

I like the knife. I've gotten, if not good at it, better. I've acquired a certain flair. On occasion I strike with fluency. From across the years I'd tell my mother I can use a knife now—not to cut an onion, no, I am the same as before, slow and plodding—but in a way she never imagined: I aim it at someone, I try to hit that person, although the knife is fake and I am only practicing.

Why? she might ask, and with the decades between us since her death, what I hear is mostly puzzlement, not accusation or regret. She's referring not only to the knife but to the fact that several times a week I put on my *gi*, that tailored, unstylish white uniform, and kick and punch. A *kiai*, to her ears, might sound like a grunt.

She doesn't ask, but I do: Would I ever cut someone? Not myself, my terrors are not those of my friend M.'s, that the knife would make its way across my wrists, although when my great-aunt, ever more frail at ninety-five, says she would rather hurt herself than me, I know what she means.

Why? my mother repeats, waiting for an answer.

* * *

No cutting, the Japanese master said during a senior black belt test when one of the students, in a symbol of victory and vanquishment, ran the practice knife over her downed opponent's wrist.

No cutting, *Kaicho*, my teacher's teacher, said again.

Even in the grand theater that the martial arts can sometimes be, he did not want to see the knife wielded for purposes of vanity or revenge.

On another stage, another day, he and his son, the heir apparent, bowed to the crowd at Lincoln Center, the son in a black ceremonial robe, the master in a plain white *gi* and frayed black belt, itself almost turned to white; and while the father retreated to the side, the son, center stage, unsheathed his sword, flashing silver in the lights, and brought it down upon the three-foot-tall Japanese daikons flanking the stage, their tops rolling to the floor, while through the crowd rolled too an audible whisper, before he, the son, turned and faced his unarmed father, who was kneeling on the ground, and after a pause—when not a sound was heard—lowered the sword toward the top of his head, and the master, rising swiftly, clapped his palms together and caught the blade between his hands; and as he unfolded them, like bird's wings, to show they were untouched, the audience, myself among them, let loose, applauding wildly.

Elective

ONE

When I was sixteen, I had minor elective surgery. My mother wanted me to have it. I went along. Call it cosmetic surgery. Plastic surgery. Aesthetic surgery. Reconstructive surgery. Rhinoplasty. I had a nose job. I had it done. Let me be straight about this from the start. It was not traumatic (or only traumatic in the sense that any surgery is traumatic: there was cutting; there was blood; there was, in the aftermath, an enormous headache). I do not regret it. If I had it to do over again, that is if I were sixteen and had it to do over again, I might do it again. But I am not sixteen. I am sixty, with a turned-up nose.

* * *

My doctor's name was Yarmo. Swarthy skin, thick hair; he was tall and magisterial. Googling him now, I come across his obituary, where by last accounts he appears to have done well for himself, an avid member of several yacht clubs. And why not? Plastic surgery is lucrative. In 2011 plastic surgeons made, on average, $270,000, compared with about half that for family practitioners. A report on mdsalaries.blogpsot.com boasts that in California, plastic surgeons could earn upward of 4 million dollars a year: "All depends on how busy you wanna get!"

When I had my surgery, we were far from rich. We lived in a modest ranch house on the North Side of Chicago. My father sold furniture out of model homes. But we were not struggling like we had been either. We no longer had to slink around Community Discount World to buy clothes, hoping we wouldn't see anyone we knew. We were coming up out of the financial doldrums. There was spare cash to invest in my appearance: braces, dermatology, plastic surgery. "Your nose is like an A-frame cottage," Dr. Mark Gorney wrote in a 1976 article on rhinoplasty. We could afford a few improvements to the infrastructure.

There was another doctor, whose name I don't remember, the one everyone in my circle was using then—a circle of middle-class, Jewish, teenage girls—but my mother chose Yarmo because she did not want my nose to look the same as all the others. Each doctor had a signature style, and you could pick the one you wanted. You could shop around. If you weren't going to have your own nose, did you want a Yarmo, for instance, or a Resnick? I took pride in this. My nose job would be different. Or was that a sop I threw to myself (throw to myself even now), something to differentiate me from the myriad other girls from whom I was no different?

Not to say that Dr. Yarmo didn't have an extensive clientele. He did. We flipped through his portfolio. Frontal views and profiles. Befores and afters. It was like looking at pictures of specialty cakes: all those marvelous concoctions. Which one should I pick? (After the surgery, would my pictures be in his book? Would other girls choose to look like me?) The girls we saw all had elective surgery, but there was one photo of a boy who'd been in a car accident. When they brought him in, Dr. Yarmo told us, the boy was a mess. It was a major reconstruction, he said.

Isn't any reconstruction major? I remember when Dr. Yarmo removed the bandages. I wasn't nervous, because I was a child who believed in the promises of adults, but my mother was terrified. What if I looked, not better—prettier, more proportional, more marriageable (that was down the line, of course), more, but not too, Gentile—but worse—misshapen, unaligned, unpretty, unmarketable (again, in the future), still too Jewish? Not to worry. The bandages came off and my nose, though swollen, was pert and sloping upward.

* * *

A nose job isn't too bloody, but it's bloody enough. They stuff your nose with packing to absorb the flow. It's not unlike the pad I wore between my legs a couple days after the surgery, when I got my period. Bleeding out of both ends: that's how, in my misery, I indelicately thought of it. Now it seems oddly fitting, to have had a nose job and my period at the same time, to have simultaneously shed blood in the name of beauty and desire. Sixteen, the age of sexual consent in many states ("Tonight's the night I've waited for / Because you're not a baby anymore," Neil Sedaka sang in "Happy Birthday Sweet Sixteen"), the age Sleeping Beauty, placed under the spell of a wicked fairy, was destined to prick her finger on the spindle of a spinning wheel and die, the age you can get your driver's license in Illinois, the age you can get married with parental consent in Illinois, the age you can donate blood in the United States, the age a girl's nose, 90 percent formed, according to most plastic surgeons, is ready for reshaping.

* * *

Susan S., Barbara A., Laurie F. These are the names, decades later, I recall. But there were more of us, a sorority of fifteen-, sixteen-, seventeen-year-olds who, between July 4 and Labor Day, when school was out, slipped into hospitals for surgery. Our brothers had been bar mitzvahed; we, bat mitzvahed or not (many families considered it unnecessary for their daughters to have a religious education), had nose jobs. My friend S., whose CV includes both a nose job and a bat mitzvah, refers to this as the scarification of the nose; along with sweet-sixteen parties, our ritual entry into womanhood. (As for me, I skipped the party and went straight to the operating room.) Some of us claimed a deviated septum, to counter accusations of vanity, but it was a cover no one took seriously; others just seemed to disappear for a few weeks, sans explanation—like girls who fled to homes for unwed mothers—only to resurface miraculously changed. All of us, when the swelling went down and the bruising faded, abandoned the guise of secrecy and proclaimed the news on our persons.

* * *

What did it look like before? A few non-Jewish friends want to know. (The Jewish ones don't ask; they've either had a nose job, considered having one, know someone who's had one, or figure it goes without saying why someone, a fellow Jew, would have one.) What they really want to know (those whose curiosity outdistances decorum—not that I mind; after all, I'm the one who's brought it up in the first place, the one, with a frisson of pleasure, who's dangled this titillating tidbit) is what was wrong with it. They want to be able to compare the bad, uncorrected nose to the good, fixed one, inasmuch as anyone can do that without having actually seen the original. Because surely I must have had a defect, a feature that needed correcting. Surely I would not have done such a thing merely for the sake of vanity, or worse, assimilation. (My friend L. can't imagine voluntarily submitting to plastic surgery, especially because she had to have surgery after a dog bit her face.) But I'm not much help in that department. I don't remember what I looked like. I don't have, lodged in memory, an internal picture of myself. Discounting the usual childhood shots, there's only one pre–nose job photo to remind me of who I was. In that photo (fourteen? fifteen?) I look prematurely professorial. Blazer, turtleneck, pageboy. And a nose that lends me a certain snobbish gravitas, a bulbous nose that turns what little I have of a smile into a sneer.

* * *

My mother'd wanted to get hers done. She'd wanted to but didn't. She had a beaky nose that trailed down her face and made her look melancholy. L., who'd seen a picture of her in my study, said she'd been a real looker. A looker. I hadn't thought of her that way. It made me, with a start, reconsider her—yes, my mother, with her high forehead and serious eyes and aquiline nose, had been beautiful. "The Lush Kid," her nickname in her high school yearbook. Winsome, my father had once called her. I suspect she didn't get her nose done because she couldn't afford it. She would have had to pay for it herself: her mother was a homemaker; her father an immigrant sign painter. And how much money did she make near the end of World War II, when she was twenty years old and working for a downtown dress manufacturer? Enough, perhaps, to buy smart clothes, but not enough for a nose job.

But maybe there were other reasons as well. In 1944, during May and June alone, 476,000 Hungarian Jews were sent to Auschwitz. On August 23, my mother's twentieth birthday, the headline on the front page of the *Chicago Daily Tribune* read YANKS GAIN 65 MI., REDS 38 / REPORT ALLIES AT BORDEAUX. Paris was liberated two days later. Perhaps, as America fought the Good War, as the war dead—Allied and Axis, military and civilian, Jew, homosexual, gypsy, Communist, Socialist, trade unionist, Free Mason, Jehovah's Witness, deaf, blind, insane, depressed, schizophrenic, epileptic—neared 70 million, it would have been indecent for Harriet Alter, a young American Jew on the West Side of Chicago, only child of Goldie and Leo Alter, to have a nose job. Or maybe not. If German Jews were having nose jobs in the years leading up to the war—and they were, for a complex mélange of reasons including vanity, mental health, and survival itself—perhaps it was no more unseemly for one of their counterparts across the ocean to consider the same. In the end, however, this is all just the speculation of the next generation, of a baby boomer who, over twenty years later, along with a significant number of her peers, was drugged and numbed and went under the knife.

TWO

My nose job has made me a snob about nose jobs. Not along ago I saw a woman in a department store who'd had one, and in a triumph of recognition, I hurried to tell Ann. I felt as though I'd outed her, a smart, savvy-looking woman with sleek dark hair and a rhinoplasty. I know your secret, I thought. I can tell. I can, in fact, spot many of them, something about the sculpted contour of the nostrils, the precise, carved look, or maybe that's mostly the old-time nose jobs, the ones from my generation. (But this woman was not my generation; she was much younger.) Some noses just don't fit. Barbara A.'s was too short. Susan S.'s, my cousin's, too snub. Mine's snub too. Maybe snub was in then, snub the standard, but it didn't suit our faces. (While snub was the fashion in 1967, snub, circa 1887, when Dr. John Orlando Roe, in Rochester, New York, introduced modern rhinoplastic techniques on pug-nosed Irish immigrants, was considered by some to be a deformity. It indicated, according to Roe, weakness of character, a view no doubt influenced by the widespread anti-Irish sentiment of the nineteenth century.) Or is the face like a palimpsest, the old face constantly showing through the new one, the old nose poking through, so I can't totally erase the picture of what was and replace it with what is? Is my old nose a shadow nose, still lurking, still big and bulbous, asserting its Semitic rights over its pert replacement?

In a horrible twist on this notion, such reclaiming is, in fact, what happens in German writer Oskar Panizza's tale *The Operated*

Jew (1893). Jewish medical student Itzig Faitel Stern is an alarming specimen of human being. His chin is drilled to his chest, his legs are bandied, his speech is a mixture of "fatty guttural noise [and] soft bawling." He waddles when he walks and gestures wildly and effeminately when talking. His mouth foams with saliva. How can he live this way? How can he, a man "who emanated directly from the stingy, indiscriminate, stifling, dirty-diapered, griping and grimacing bagatelle of his family upbringing," make his way through the chaste and noble corridors of Heidelberg society? He can't. And so he submits to a series of grueling procedures: multiple surgeries to straighten his bones, speech therapy, a four-week drug regimen to lend his skin a Teutonic tint, hair coloring and straightening, and lastly, to complete the job, eight liters of Christian blood (a reference to the infamous charge of blood libel). Voila! Meet Siegfried Freudenstern, who, thus transformed (apparently no one realizes this is the former Faitel Stern), is ready to take a German wife and propagate the race. Only something goes awry at the wedding. Siegfried has too much to drink (Jews, of course, can't hold their liquor), and under the enormous pressures of disguise and conformity, and with no small amount of lip-smacking vindictiveness, his cankerous Jewish self explodes. The changes, never really permanent in the first place, come undone. His speech takes on its former patterns ("I vant you shood know dat I'm a human bing jost as good for sumtink as any ov you!"); his posture assumes its "crippled looking compulsive formation"; his hair curls and turns black; and he collapses in a pool of vomit. Itzig Faitel Stern. Operated, manipulated, mocked, destroyed, he is once and for always The Jew.

THREE

Until recently, I thought Jimmy Durante was Jewish. Durante. The son of an immigrant Italian barber. Christened James Francis Durante. Grew up on New York's Lower East Side. An altar boy at Saint Malachy's. I thought he was Jewish because of his nose. I was disappointed to find out that he wasn't. I'd wanted him to live up to my expectation of a big-nosed Jew, a lovable wise guy I could claim as one of my own; and if I couldn't claim him as one of my own, then at least I'd point out that he grew up among the Jewish garment workers of the Lower East Side, as if, ridiculously, their Jewishness and their nozzles could somehow have rubbed off on him.

What does this say about me? That I've succumbed to certain assumptions about My People? That I, a former big-nosed Jew, am full of tired preconceptions? Outsize pride? Am I claiming the same kind of in-house privilege that leads Blacks, when speaking of their own, to say *nigger*, or gays *queer*?

Is the iconic nose iconic because it's Jewish?

Durante, Catholic and not one of my people, nicknamed himself Schnozzola. Schnozzola/Schnozzle/Schnoz. Probably an alteration of the Yiddish *snoyts*, "snout, muzzle," from the German *Schnauze* (the German Schnauzer, a vigilant, sober dog, very loyal to its handler, not led astray by bribes). And/or the Yiddish *shnabl*, "beak." Durante reportedly said that after his schoolmates mercilessly taunted him, he'd "go home and cry. I made up my mind never to hurt anybody else, no matter what. I never made jokes about anybody's big ears, crossed eyes, or their stuttering." Instead, he made jokes about himself. "My nose isn't big," he said. "I just happen to have a very small head."

Milton Berle, on the other hand, *was* Jewish (born Milton Berlinger, son of Sarah and Moses Berlinger), with a noteworthy nose, or at least a nose he deemed noteworthy enough to have bobbed, as he put it (*bob*: to cut short; dock; often with *off*: as, to bob or bob off a horse's tail). One report says he broke his nose during a comedy routine, but Berle, in his autobiography, makes no mention of this. All he says is that the tip turned down when he smiled and he decided to fix it. Pleased with his new look, he gave nose jobs as presents to friends, one of whom, in a strange bit of only-in-America nomenclature, dubbed him Santa Schnozo in return. "I cut off my nose to spite my race," Berle joked during his routine.

* * *

One Rosh Hashanah I went to Manny's diner for breakfast and ordered pigs in a blanket. I'm a hand-wringing kind of Jew: I was taking the day off from work for the Jewish holiday and eating sausages wrapped in pancakes and feeling uneasy about the whole arrangement. About my truancy, the pork, my observance/nonobservance of the holiday. I had no plans to go to temple. That word is a holdover from my childhood, when we called this place we rarely went to *temple*, and a holdover from the Temple that used to stand on the Temple Mount in Jerusalem. I took the day off from work because I didn't feel right about working on the holiday (although I didn't feel right about not working, either) and because my boss, owner of the print shop where I ran the offset press, was also Jewish.

Eating the sausages, I experienced a queasy pleasure. They were forbidden (*trayf*, impure, not Kosher), but they were greasy and good. They felt more forbidden because it was the holiday and I was making a feeble attempt to observe it. Forbidden? I'd always eaten forbidden food. In our house it was not forbidden. In restaurants it was savored. Shrimp scampi, ribs, egg rolls, BLT's. Although we'd always shied away from ham and pork chops. That seemed to cross some line. There was *trayf* but good, and then there was too *trayf*. Ham and pork chops were too *trayf*. On this day, this Rosh Hashanah, I slathered the pancakes and sausages with syrup. The sweet and the savory together. Possibly I read the newspaper as I ate. Then someone I knew came into the diner. Someone about whom, all these years later, I can hardly conjure up a single detail. But in that instant I felt caught. Busted. A true truant. A Jew on the lam. She must have said something about my not being at work that day, and I must have said something about the Jewish holiday. Because then she said, *I didn't know you were Jewish.* And I thought, must have thought, think now, *What did she mean by that?* Certainly there was an awkward silence. *Well, I am,* I said, said self-deprecatingly and defiantly at the same time. The self-deprecation and the defiance seemed to cover all the bases. Shame, embarrassment, confusion, defensiveness, anger, pride. Perhaps I added an offhand laugh. Can't you tell? I thought. What's it to you? And now that you know?

Am I being too harsh? Ungenerous? Did I misunderstand her? Valid questions, but another tugs at me more urgently. Why didn't she know? Why didn't she recognize me? I want people to know I'm Jewish. I want to be taken for who I am. I bear the signs of assimilation: an indeterminate surname—when my father and his brother changed their name from Shinitzky to Shinner, the change, in and of itself, could have been read as a possible sign of Jewishness. In 1922, as part of an effort to lower the percentage of Jewish students, Harvard revised its application form. One of the new questions was "What change, if any, has been made since birth in your own name or that of your father? (Explain fully)"—an improbably Irish-sounding first name, an omnivorous diet, a nonreligious lifestyle, a snub nose. I didn't get a nose job to look less Jewish. (But isn't that what everyone says, patients and practitioners alike? "I wanted to look prettier and my nose was a sight in any language, but I wasn't trying to hide my origin," singer and actor Fanny Brice once protested. Or, as Drs. Dennis P. Cirillo and Mark Rubenstein put it in *The Complete Book of Cosmetic Facial Surgery,* "If your daughter does wish to belittle her background, other signs of this intention would, no doubt, have appeared by now.") I didn't get a nose job for any particular reason I could have articulated at age sixteen, except, like Brice, to look better. I got a nose job mostly because it was expected of me. Expected of me, particularly, and expected of someone like me: young, female, Jewish, with fair-to-middling, meaning subject-to-improvement, looks, in the middle of the twentieth century. Small wonder, perhaps, that my acquaintance at Manny's hadn't tagged my identity. Had the evidence been erased from my face, surgically removed? Would my big and bulbous nose have delivered the news?

* * *

The Jew's nose, my nose (my former nose, or some rendition thereof), has long existed in the popular imagination. Over the centuries it's been described as humped, hooked, hawkish, club shaped, crooked, convex, and in the children's book *Der Giftpilz* (*The Poison Mushroom*), published by Nazi propagandist Julius Streicher, "like the number six." "It indicates considerable Shrewdness in worldly matters; a deep insight into character, and facility of turning that insight to profitable account," wrote George Jabet, aka Eden Warwick, in *Notes on Noses*, a nineteenth-century physiognomy text. This nose, real, satirized, or an anti-Semitic construction, has circulated as common currency. In an unintentionally comic attempt to refute it, JewishEncyclopedia.com cites a study which found that among modern Eastern European Jews, the majority of noses are not arched or hooked but "straight, or what is popularly known as Greek."

Some version of the Jew's nose exists in my mind as well. My friend M., who herself had a nose job and is resentful about it, or resentful of the pressures that forced her into it, not the least of which was an insistent mother, recently went to Israel to visit relatives. I have long admired M.'s nose, which is straight, strong, and subtly authoritative, and was surprised to find out she'd had it done. I was surprised because it looks, post–nose job, Jewish. In talking about her trip to Israel, about family relations, the West Bank wall, the occupation, amid all this parsing of the complexities of our time, M. stopped for a second and laughed and said, in a voice suggesting she might admit this only in the company of friends, It was a pleasure to see all those distinctive noses.

FOUR

Did M.'s nose job do the job? Did mine? What do we, who find ourselves allied in the strange confederacy of nose-fixers, aspire to? A nose that conforms to a facial angle of thirty-three degrees and is the approximate angle of Venus de Milo's nose, which was the feminine ideal suggested by fin-de-siècle German Jewish surgeon Jacques Joseph, a pioneer of modern plastic surgery? (For a man, the preferred angle is slightly bigger, implying that a man's face can, and indeed should, carry a more prominent nose.)

What about passing? Dr. Joseph's first rhinoplasty patient, a man of unknown origin whose large nose had led to public ridicule and subsequent depression, indicated that after the surgery his distress subsided and he was able to move around unnoticed. Sixteen-year-old Adolphine Schwarz, another of Joseph's patients, had her nose done in 1934, a year after the Nazis came into power. Her older brother, "suffer [ing] from a Jewish nose," had already undergone the operation. "I . . . had a nose that bothered me, especially after the Hitler regime started," Schwarz noted. "So it was decided that I too should have my nose reshaped." Schwarz's nose job, of course, did not protect her. Four years later, she and her family were forced to flee Munich and their famous restaurant, whose patrons had included Albert Einstein and Charlie Chaplin. Her parents died in Auschwitz, while Schwarz and her husband eventually resettled in the United States.

For some, such as Milton Berle, the stakes were much less high. He hoped a nose job would help boost his career. "I liked the new look so much," he wrote in his autobiography, "I decided it would make all the difference when—and if—the next shot at the movies came." Indeed, the next shot came shortly after, in 1941, with *Tall, Dark, and Handsome*, which won an Academy Award for Best Original Screenplay.

Is a nose job successful if the person didn't want it in the first place? If she's indifferent about how it looks but unhappy with what it means? M. doesn't say whether she is happy with her nose, but she is clearly troubled by her nose job. Troubled, I suspect, by the prevailing social attitudes which judged her original nose unattractive, unfeminine, and, of course, demonstrably Jewish. Troubled as well by her understandable inability, as a teenager, to stand up to those judgments. For my part, if I'm troubled neither by my nose job nor my nose, I'm uneasy with my passive acceptance of the anonymity it has given me. Anonymity lets others fill in the blanks. *I didn't know you were Jewish*, my acquaintance at Manny's diner had said. *You don't look Jewish*, she might as well have said. On what was she basing her assessment? Sure, I want to be taken for who I am, but like Adolphine Schwartz and all the others who "suffered from a Jewish nose," I don't want to suffer too much for it.

* * *

What do the rabbis have to say about nose jobs? I have never been in the habit of consulting rabbis, except in times of death, when I've looked to them for last farewells—even if, in the manner of Durante, they've had not much more to say than "Goodnight Mrs. Calabash, wherever you are." But, as is also my habit, I seem to be interested in their prescripts after the fact. I guess I want to know where I'd fit in, if I'd fit in at all, where my actions fall in their grand accounting.

As it turns out, the rabbis approve. They give a nod to my nose job. The Jews are a practical people. There are laws that govern all aspects of Jewish life ("one must not walk 'four cubits' upon rising in the morning until after having poured water three times . . . upon the fingers of each hand alternately [so as to rid the body completely of the evil spirits that entered the body upon going to sleep at night]"), and then there are the allowances. Four laws, in particular, are relevant to nose jobs: those that prohibit indulging in vanity, wounding the body, endangering one's life, and tampering with God's handiwork. (In an odd and macabre twist of this idea, neo-Nazi Jonathan Preston Haynes murdered plastic surgeon Martin Sullivan in 1993 because Sullivan, by operating on patients and altering their God-given, presumably Semitic features, "dilute[ed] . . . Aryan beauty.") But these mandates may be set aside, according to various twentieth-century Jewish legal scholars, if a woman's nose—her deformity, as Rabbi Immanuel Jakobovits puts it—"make[s] it difficult for [her] to find a matrimonial partner or to maintain a happy relationship with her husband." Relief of emotional pain overrides the ban on wounding the body, adds Rabbi Yaakov Breisch. The anguish of not being able to find, or keep, a suitable partner, Rabbis Menashe Klein and Yitzchak Yaakov Weiss concur, is sufficient reason to allow cosmetic surgery. If surgery helps a girl find a mate, it is self-healing, not self-wounding, says Rabbi Moshe Feinstein.

In other words, make an appointment.

As for men, the rationale is different but the outcome the same. Deuteronomy 22:5 reads: "A woman shall not wear a man's garment, neither shall a man put on a woman's garment; it is an abomination before God." Men cannot dress like women, masquerade as women, take up female behaviors, be one of the girls. Therefore, in a world where cosmetic surgery is typically associated with women and vanity thought to be an especially female and corrupting trait, the rabbis might be expected to rule against nose jobs for men. But more pressing social factors are at play. What about a man's role as provider? (He was a good provider, my great-aunt used to say about her philandering husband.) A man may have a nose job, Rabbi Jakobovits argues, if his deformity prevents him "from playing a constructive role in society and . . . maintaining himself and his family in decent comfort." In this view, a nose job may be the ticket to a middle-class life, a life of decent comfort; and although that seems laughable at first, or it did to me, research shows the rabbi might be right. According to a 2005 study, below-average-looking men suffer a "plainness penalty" in the labor market: they earn 9 percent less than their better-looking counterparts. Good-looking men, says the study, get more job offers, higher starting salaries, and bigger raises. Looks pay.

FIVE

There is another picture, my post–nose job picture, my after shot. It was taken at a sweet sixteen. In my tight-fitting dress and new nose, I'm practically bursting out of the picture. It is 1967, ten years before the premiere of *Roots*, five years before *Ms.* magazine debuted, three years before Kent State, two years before I went to college, one year before Barbra Streisand—perhaps the most famous Jew who never had a nose job, whose nose was described in *Ladies Home Companion* as "overly-prominent," in *Time* as a "shrine," in *Newsweek* as "absurd," in *Life* like "a witch['s]," in *Saturday Evening Post* like "an eagle['s]," and in *Life* again as "like Everest, There"—starred in *Funny Girl*, a film about Fanny Brice. In the photo, my skin is shiny, my nose is swollen, my smile is slightly pleading. My dress is the color of well-fertilized grass. Next to me is Barbara A., the daughter of Holocaust survivors who tried to flee Poland on the back of a horse cart, but were caught and sent to a camp. She hasn't had her nose done yet, hasn't had the hump on her bridge, inherited from her father, chiseled down. But she will, by the time *Funny Girl* opens and Streisand, as Best Actress, wins an Academy Award.

The Fitting(s)

A few years ago I went shopping for new brassieres. I bought five, although there was no discount for buying in bulk: two Warner's Fit To Be Tried SuperCross, two Fit To Be Tried HiddenPowers, and one Anita's Big Cup Beauty Comfort Bra, for a total of $173.88. I got them at Schwartz's, a store I was familiar with: over forty years before, my mother had taken me to the original Schwartz's, two bus rides away, for my first bras, and I'd gone periodically ever since. We rode, first the #82 Kimball bus, and then the #155 Devon Avenue bus, before disembarking at Rockwell, in the heart of the Rogers Park shopping district on Chicago's Far North Side. You could get anything you wanted on Devon: sour-cream rolls, culottes, high chairs, heels, Seder plates, recliners, an eye exam, knee-highs, girdles. Schwartz's Intimate Apparel, cramped and claustrophobic, was on the corner.

On this day, however, I got on the Edens Expressway and drove twenty-five minutes—over twelve miles—to Wilmette, an affluent northern suburb where Schwartz's, spacious and well lit, is now located. I felt a hint of furtiveness about the excursion, as if I had to hide the fact that I was, for a few hours, leaving the present and slipping into the past. And who would notice? Ann, who might be interested, was at work, and no one else would even pretend. Still, I was soft-pedaling my anticipation. These little forays into the past are often self-indulgent.

Schwartz's: serving the foundation needs of Chicago-area women for over half a century.

I got out of the car and locked the door.

From the cedar-chip-covered divide in the parking lot, one lone red tulip struggled to bloom. In the window, heavily eye-shadowed mannequins lolled around in pink and green lounging pajamas, pink terrycloth robes, lacy apple-green camisoles, mauve panties. Wilmette Commons. I went there, not just to buy a bra, which you can do at any number of places, but to be fitted for one. I am, so it seems, unfit to fit myself. I need an expert, a sharp-eyed, sharp-tongued, no-nonsense woman (she herself is ironclad) with manicured nails who, from around her neck, takes a school-bus-yellow tape measure, limp from years of usage, circles it under your breasts to measure your rib cage, circles it a second time across your nipples to measure your cup size, and comes back minutes later—all while you're left in the dressing room shirtless, braless, foolish, and freezing—with five or six possibilities slung over her arm, and says, Here, try these on.

You are the good daughter. You do as you are told.

Or do you? Sorry to disappoint. But you were disappointing from the very beginning, from the moment, in the dressing room, when you said no underwires—*sans armature*, on the Warner's Fit To Be Tried label, which, in retrospect, seems to have given your position more authority because, well, anything in French sounds more persuasive, a view Warner's, an American company headquartered in Connecticut, apparently holds as well—because you did not want to wear something so unyielding, and you could tell by the way the saleswoman looked at the size of your breasts (36C), by the way she *assessed* them, that she thought you were sadly, pathetically, mistaken. And now that the saleswoman has brought her picks—two pink, two beige, a white—you've become contrary again: it turns out that you do not want a pink bra, no matter how good the fit. It's not that you don't like pink. You have a lovely wool sweater that's candidly pink, a well-worn pink Key West T-shirt (a hand-me-down from a beloved friend), and right now, outside the upstairs window, the redbud tree is dazzlingly pink. But you do not want pink undergarments. Undergarments, in your view, say something secret and telling about you. You cannot imagine wearing a pink bra in your *dojo* locker room where, in front of your training partners, it could undermine your already shaky self-image as an athlete. So you screw up your courage and indicate your lack of enthusiasm. You bear up under the saleswoman's gaze, a mix of disapproval and contempt, a second time. You put the two pink bras aside and try on the beige and the white.

But still there's the matter of uplift. She wants to give you more than you're interested in. She yanks on the straps until your breasts feel as high as your throat, until you feel as though you've swallowed them. It is, perhaps, no coincidence that the French word for "bra," *soutien-gorge*, literally translates as "throat support." "Tits on a tray," says one of the characters in Manuel Puig's *Kiss of the Spiderwoman*, referring to an actress in a strapless gown with reinforced cups, whose breasts looked like they were propped on a platter. Gently, so as not to offend, you ask the saleswoman to loosen the straps. Another look of censure or pity, and this time she abandons you altogether. She leaves you to try on the bras by yourself. Which is not what you've come for. You've come for precisely what you've gotten—bossy, hands-on treatment—and now you're no longer getting it.

You have failed. In this interaction between novice and expert, petitioner and petitioned, the bra fitter has performed her role to a T, she has perfectly and imperiously acted her part; you are the one, with your equivocations and refusals, with your *opinions*, who has fallen short.

Why do this? Why submit to, indeed seek out, a situation that's inevitably humiliating, disappointing, or both? I went to Schwartz's to recapture an experience I had never liked in the first place. I was nostalgic for something I'd initially abhorred. I was eleven years old when my mother took me there, eleven, thirteen, fifteen, and the saleswoman—steel-plated bosom, platinum nails—plumped and lifted and jiggled and otherwise handled my breasts. I was horrified, and embarrassed, and, in any case, in thrall. My mother let her do this? Indeed, my mother, who didn't drive, who lugged us on not one but two buses, delivered me to the sacrifice. She and the fitter were in league. Mothers of a certain kind, of my mother's kind—middle-class, middle-aged, who believed in experts—handed their daughters (and themselves) over to professionals. Seamstresses, hairdressers, decorators, bra fitters. There was a chair in the tiny dressing room where my mother could sit and hold the flung and discarded articles, and a mirror in front of us that captured the whole alarming spectacle.

Yet I don't totally trust my account. I wonder if I'm distorting the truth. Yes, I did chafe at the bra-fitting experience, at the shame, the handling, the humiliation, much as I chafed at the rambunctiousness of my body itself, which seemed to bulge and bleed of its own accord. But while I might have been too pimpled, too developed—as well as too bookish, too gullible, too polite—with an egg-shaped birthmark on my leg that a classmate mistook for a smudge of dirt, she and all the others, I was sure, had never been to a bra fitter. That set me apart, and though I was already set apart, this experience conferred merit. There was something honorific about it. Consider this: The bra fitter was complimentary. She liked my breasts. She might have said they were perky. She didn't deride them. And she was a world removed from the bullies of fourth and fifth grade, the three or four members of IHP, the I HATE PEGGY club, who followed me home from school, pulled on my bra straps, and chanted IHP behind my back.

* * *

Schwartz's sold swimwear as well as undergarments, and at nineteen I went there for a bikini. Ten years earlier, I'd sung "Itsy Bitsy Teenie Weenie Yellow Polka-Dot Bikini" in a Brownie talent show, dressed in a stiff brown uniform, scarf, and knee socks and warbling away in my false falsetto. All the mothers applauded. Lyricist Paul Vance wrote the song after watching his two-year old bikini-clad daughter waddle along the shoreline. This would be the first time, however, that I would be wearing one. I was going for a semester in Costa Rica and needed a bathing suit. I don't remember buying the suit, but I remember the suit itself. It was tropical: red, yellow, green, loud like a parrot. The day before I left on my flight to San José, I rode my bicycle around the neighborhood wearing it, preening my feathers as if the parrot had escaped. I was about to escape, off on a trip that would take me ten degrees shy of the equator, and although I would eventually return to Chicago, to my neighborhood, I did wear the bikini on a beach in Costa Rica, cracking open coconuts fallen from palm trees, sleeping in a beach hut. On the farm where I lived there, picking coffee and oranges, they called me *Gordita*, "little fat one," not because I was fat so much as well rounded, and it was meant as flattery, an endearment. But it meant something else when I was walking down the street of a dusty rural town—a *gringa* in a short skirt, with spare change—and a man coming toward me thrust his hand in my crotch. *Gordita, gringa, Norteamericana*, he gestured with contempt.

* * *

Once, in the spirit of independence, I defected and went to Marshall Field's to buy a bra. This was the period when I wore bulky down jackets and button-down shirts and, in my mother's eyes, tried to look as unattractive as possible. I had come out several years before, and although I read books such as *Lesbianism and the Women's*

Movement and *Flaunting It!* I had little inclination to go braless. In the lingerie department at Field's no one waited on me, handled me, measured me; no one came into the dressing room with her expert selections and ladled me into the cups. I picked out the bras myself, from the rack. I looked for the familiar names: Bali, Olga, Warner's. I slung them over my wrist. A saleswoman, if she appeared at all, appeared discreetly. Did I need any help? None, I assured her. We were both relieved. I slipped into the dressing room and tried the bras on. Here my confidence, shored up by rebellion but not much else, fell away. I did not have the eye of a bra fitter. I was looking at my partially clothed body in a full-length mirror, my body that, according to the diary I briefly and earnestly kept at age fourteen, had measured 34-24-35, and I could not look at it the way a professional bra fitter might, with the eye of commerce. The bra fitter would appraise the bra; I, however, appraised the body. There was, in this once-over, the usual catalogue of flaws: large hips, dimpled thighs, bad posture. Standing before the mirror, hopelessly trying on one style and then another, I needed a third-party arbiter. I needed the fitter, not only for her expertise in fitting, but also for her ability to deflect attention from the body and back to the bra.

By now the enterprise was tainted. I gathered up my lackluster choices and made my way back to the cash register. The saleswoman rang me up. Did you find everything you wanted? she asked. Yes, I nodded miserably, carrying off the ill-fitting purchases.

* * *

At thirty-nine, I returned to the fold. My parents were dead, my brother was getting married, and I needed a bra. By then I had a lover of thirteen years, two cats, and a mortgage. I was a partner in a soon-to-be defunct consulting business. It was left to me to tie my brother's cummerbund and walk him down the aisle to the *chuppah*. Ann and I went to Schwartz's, which, like everything else, had changed. It had relocated from Devon. The Jews had moved away—as I had moved away—and the store had followed their (but not my) suburban migration. In Wilmette, Schwartz's was across the street from Piser Chapel, an affiliate of the funeral home that had, over the years, buried both my parents. Piser, originally located just blocks from Devon, had followed the Jews on the final lap of their journey.

We were waited on by an African-American saleswoman in a cardigan sweater, wool skirt, sturdy shoes. She took the standard measurements and came back with her picks. She was solid in stature and manner. Kind, competent. Almost, but not quite, apologetic in tone. I was not Scarlett O'Hara and she was not Mammy and this was not 1861, when Mammy tightened Scarlett's corset around her seventeen-inch waist and said, "Ain' nobody got a wais' lak mah lamb," but I can't help, from this remove, thinking about history. I can't help thinking of my own childhood, when we employed an African-American woman, Willie Esther, to clean our house twice a month. She got down on all fours to wash the kitchen floor, knees on a crumbling rubber mat, and as I made my way to the refrigerator I skirted the slick spots so as not to undo her efforts. She had a much-loved son who'd gone to New York as an actor, and wiping the floor, she talked about his career. When my mother died, Willie paid a condolence call, but then I lost track of her, and not knowing when she died, I never did the same. If I wasn't uncomfortable at Schwartz's—and I don't remember if I was—I'm uncomfortable now, remembering this. I'm uncomfortable remembering that the Yiddish word for the color black, *shvartz*, gave rise to the word *shvartze*, a derogatory term for a black person. Perhaps the Jew who passed through Ellis Island in the early twentieth century, after, let's say, the pogrom at Kishinev, was given the name Schwartz because of his own swarthy skin. Perhaps in Kishinev he was a dry-goods merchant. Who eventually made his way to Chicago. And opened up a small sundries shop, where buxom immigrant women, speaking little English, flocked for their foundations.

That day at Schwartz's, years ago, I was disappointed because the saleswoman did not correspond to the bra fitter I remembered. The bra fitter pulled from the fluff of memory. She was not like ninety-five-year old Selma Koch of New York City, interviewed on NPR, who said, "Bras are really my specialty. I never had to try six brassieres on a customer. Two was plenty. . . . I knew in a minute what was right, finished, buy it, out." Or Ida Rosenthal, founder of Maidenform and codesigner of the first bra with cups, who said in a 1960 *Newsweek* interview: "Quality we give them. Delivery we give them. I add personality." Tough, brash, pushy, Jewish. My bra fitter. My brother was getting married, my parents were gone, and though I would not be so reductive as to say I sought out some remnant of my childhood in the weeks before the wedding, I would not be so quick to reject that idea either. I am not above sentiment. In my new bra, under my new clothes (an outfit my mother would have surely approved of: a low-cut blouse and black silk pants embroidered with tiny pearls), before the assembled guests, I gave a toast to the newly married couple and said, if not what my parents might have said, perhaps what they might have liked to hear, and then we drank.

* * *

Now it's cold in the dressing room. I feel, ridiculously, like an orphan. I've been abandoned. The bra fitter, whom I drove away, is out front, courting other customers. I remember when I was eight, shopping with my mother in Marshall Field's and afraid to put one foot on the escalator because the other would remain stuck at the top and I would be split in half. My mother grew impatient with me. Without a word, she left me to fend for myself at the top of the stairs and took the elevator instead.

In a dressing room across the aisle, a woman who sounds younger than I am is trying on bathing suits. Her voice is desperate. She is trying not to whine. She is, as I imagine it, in a primordial struggle with her body, which confronts her, like a second body, in the mirror. There is the body she inhabits, the one that has made love, borne children, nursed them; and then there is this body, the one in the mirror, the renegade body, which never fails to surprise and alarm her. It has taken on a shape she doesn't recognize.

Now she says to the saleswoman, Does it come in another color? I don't know, she says. I just don't like red. What do you think?

* * *

Is it possible to talk about bras without talking about breasts? I count them up. I have two. Ann has one, N. has one, S. has one (although she plans on two after her treatment is done), my mother, when she died (of something else), had one, my grandmother (also dead of something else) one, B. (diagnosed two months after Ann and now dead) one. *To the four of us and our six breasts*, N. had said, raising a glass of wine in a toast shortly after Ann's mastectomy. Two couples, four friends, six breasts. The woman on the other side of this wall has two, but she's not happy with them. She has indentations on her shoulders from the weight of them, the burden, the ceaseless sagging, the heavy load. She tells the fitter this, her fitter, not mine; she tells the fitter that one breast is larger than the other (not uncommon, the fitter says), that she had a lumpectomy eight years ago (the way she says it sounds like just yesterday), and that she hopes the fitter will be able to do something, lighten her burden, relieve her load; she implores the fitter, and her voice (like her breasts) is ponderous, mournful, pleading, but the fitter is unsympathetic, dismissive, scornful even, perhaps because she's seen everything, she's seen worse (and who know what scars she herself hides), and the indentations are part and parcel, commonplace, nothing to be done.

* * *

A week after her mastectomy, my mother went to Schwartz's for a prosthesis. She couldn't go soon enough. Who would want me? she had said, suggesting that if she were ever back on the open market (i.e., if my father died first, which, according to the actuarial tables, was a statistical probability, or had been, before her diagnosis), she'd be nothing but damaged goods. I drove us there. We walked down an aisle of lingerie and lounging pajamas. A fitter greeted us. We were not ushered into a dressing room. My mother did not try anything on. The transaction took place at the counter. There was only the soft light, the muted voices, the packaging. Elegant and pristine, like a box of chocolates. And in the center, swaddled in silky fabric, the prosthesis, nestled like a special treat. It was soft, the fitter said, durable; it molded to the shape of your body. (It would, for the remaining six years of my mother's life, sit on her dresser every night, a glistening jelly mold.)

But it didn't really matter what she said. We were buying anyway.

* * *

My mother had a prophylactic mastectomy. That's how they (The Doctors, The Medical Establishment, but in fact there was only one doctor, Dr. Southwick, and he wore a bow tie) referred to it. Over a period of years, she had three lumps, three biopsies. The first two were benign, the third revealed precancerous cell changes. Not cancer. Not not cancer. Better to cut it off, the dapper doctor said, but not in so many words. Better to be safe.

Safe, my mother thought, must have thought. She complied.

My mother was a combination of prim and prurient. *Prophylactic* was the word she used for condom. Keep your legs crossed, she said. Men like sex better than women, she claimed. Yet she would laugh, suggestively, at a word like *cherry*. She would make it into something lewd. At the dinner table, in front of my lover (Was it Passover? Were we eating dessert? Was there some mention of a chocolate-covered cherry?), she made me blush. She enlisted the lover (Ann: at that point we'd only been together a year), whom she didn't even like—pinstripe suit, broad shoulders, small breasts, Why does she look so masculine? my mother had remarked on another occasion—for her side. I became the prudish, uptight daughter, she the hip, free mother with her cohort of convenience. *Cherry.* Neither could suppress a laugh.

For good measure, the doctor biopsied the other, presumably healthy breast during the mastectomy and reported, on his post-surgical visit, that it was fine. He thought this was good news, but my mother's mind was on what was lost, not found: she asked, a small smile on her lips, Can I have it back?

* * *

Finally the fitter returns. She's cheerful, as though there's been no rift between us. I try to get her back in my corner. I ply her with self-deprecating charm. I show her my shabby, frayed bra, the one I've worn to the store—bits of forlorn nylon escaping from the seams, whatever uplift it once provided now gone—in order to establish buyer-seller rapport, in order to say, *See, I belong here, I need you.* I apologize for the bra, for myself, and she nods, smiles, says it is the kind of thing your mother told you not to wear in case you were ever in a car accident; and even though I'm not sure that I expected reassurance, so we could bond about my miserable bra even as we made light of its miserableness—*It's not so bad; believe me, I've seen worse*—or that I set this up so she would agree with me, so she could smile and be reseated on her throne, when she does agree I feel diminished. A fool, in her shredded undergarment. An orphan once again.

* * *

The fitter, it turns out, knows her breasts. Knows her merchandise. All the bras fit. Let me see, she says, tugging and lifting. Looking in the mirror and appraising. Mmm-hmm, she says, neither surprised nor pleased. Matter-of-fact. One of the bras, the Anita Big

Cup Beauty Comfort, costs twice as much as the others (almost sixty dollars) and twice as much as I've ever spent on a bra. Expensive, I say, glancing at the tag, at the picture of the wholesome, rosy-cheeked, Nordic-looking blonde I don't resemble. She suggests a kind of good-natured, robust sexuality contained, but barely, by her Big Cup Beauty Comfort bra: take off the bra and she becomes a tiger. It's a good product, the fitter says with the same noncommittal expression on her face as before, and I have to admit that the *café con leche* bra secures my breasts admirably. This sales technique, I later learn, is known as trading up. Bring the customer two or three comparably styled items of varied quality, in the hope that the most expensive one will win her over and produce a sale. But I feel had. I can't spend sixty dollars apiece on bras, not when I need four or five; and Schwartz's doesn't have it in white, the color I prefer, even though the fitter tells me that white shows under clothes (I've worn it my whole adult life) and the *café con leche* (called Skin on the Anita website, where all the models look like sultry Caucasians) never shows, you can wear it under anything. Besides, but I don't tell the fitter this, the Anita Big Cup Beauty Comfort, with its wide straps and reinforced stitching, is serviceable (never mind the eager blonde) and I don't want serviceable, which in my mind is linked to *matronly*, a word, with its undertones of class privilege and stolidity and aging, my mother always used with derision. I want, like my locker-room cohort S.—who doesn't worry about her image as an athlete, or not enough to eschew pink or uplift—sexy. Or at least the suggestion thereof.

Instead, I get dressed, put on my own frayed but familiar undergarment, and assemble my choices, among which is one (but only one) Anita Big Cup Beauty Comfort, with its sturdy though slightly demoralizing fit and big, unwieldy name.

* * *

This is the season of Passover. At the counter, the fitter rings me up while another saleswoman chats about her holiday meal. Are you ready? the fitter says after getting the total, assuming, I suppose, that I need to be braced for the expense. But I'm prepared; such support, I've long known, is expensive. Besides, if you prorate the total over the number of years I've gone without buying a bra, the expense is negligible. Almost twenty-nine dollars a year. Rib-eye roast, eggs with chopped onion, stuffing for the bird—which could have used just one more egg, the other saleswoman says. The fitter gives a sideways nod as she waits for the approval on my charge. As for me, I'm going to my friend M.'s for the Seder. Every year M. and her partner open up their dining room table, add a hodgepodge of card tables and chairs, cover them all with tablecloths, cook a chicken and some soup, chop apples and walnuts for *haroset*, and invite their Jewish and non-Jewish friends, all of whom are happy for the opportunity to share a meal, bring a dish to the table, drink red wine, eat bitter herbs, and talk about leading the slaves out of Egypt. The Haggadah was lovingly put together by M. et al., and is earnest and political. It makes us feel good about ourselves, if not about the world. We recite the ten plagues: blood, frogs, lice, wild beasts, blight, boils, hail, locusts, darkness, slaying of the firstborn, and solemnly add some of our own: hunger, poverty, breast cancer, war, racism, homophobia, substandard housing, rape, ignorance, homelessness. We read the words of Anne Frank, "I keep my ideals, because in spite of everything I still believe that people are really good at heart," and then debate—briefly—whether we believe this is true. People are capable of anything, both good and evil, someone says, and that produces a smattering of consideration before we move on to the fourth and final cup of wine. This year her partner is out of town, so M. is doing the Seder on her own. Ann and I are bringing chocolate macaroons from Angel Food Bakery.

The fitter gives me the receipt to sign, and I scribble my name across the bottom. Lending my mark to the exchange feels conspiratorial. As though the fitter and I are allied against my other self, that woman we've left behind in the dressing room to sort through her opinions. We've come to an agreement. She hands me the plastic bag with my purchases. What does it matter that I eschewed her advice? What does it matter that she abandoned me? I'm leaving with five well-fitted undergarments. The fitter has added to her daily receipts.

As I'm about to leave, a twenty-something woman heads toward the fitting rooms with a bunch of bikinis strung over her arm. Can I help you? my fitter says, and I feel a pang of jealousy. I'm not even out the door and already she's moved on. She's ready to latch on to someone else. The young woman, dark-haired, determined, and with an air about her that suggests she knows precisely what she wants, declines. Is it possible my fitter looks, for a moment, crestfallen? Is it possible I feel, for a moment, buoyed by her discomfort? Don't be silly, I tell myself, opening the door. I secure the grip on my purchases. Later the bra fitter will go to her Seder and I'll go to M.'s for mine, and we'll each, in the sputtering glow of candles, dip a sprig of parsley in salt water to symbolize the tears of those enslaved, and wash it down with wine.

In the parking lot, I give a passing glance to Piser across the street and aim my car toward the city. I take the streets this time; I don't go back the way I came. On this route, I pass the neighborhood I grew up in. The fish market is gone, the jewelry store too. Bunny Hutch, where my brother used to serve up hot dogs, remains. I don't stop, but if I did I'd see, like I have on previous occasions, that our ranch house, with its Japanese garden out front, purple painted rocks, and curlicued, wrought-iron railing, all put in by the current owners, looks nothing like it did before.

Berenice's Hair

The Tantrics said the forces of creation and destruction lay in the binding and unbinding of a woman's hair. The Syrians said a woman who combed her hair on the Eve of Holy Sunday consorted with werewolves. The Slavs said the *vili*, or female spirits, hid in the water and made rain by combing their hair. The Scots said women should refrain from combing their hair at night when their brothers were at sea, because that could raise a storm and sink the boats. In Laos, the wife of an elephant hunter was forbidden to cut her hair in order not to sever the ropes restraining the elephant. The Navajo prohibited a woman from washing her hair while her husband was out hunting lest he come home empty-handed. The Punjabi said a woman should not wash her hair on Thursday or Sunday, because "the house would lose money and people would tell us lies." The Romans said that strands of a woman's hair made fine strings for bows against the Gauls. Berenice, wife of Egyptian king Ptolemy III, made an offering of her hair to Aphrodite, for her husband's safe return from war. Upon his homecoming, her hair appeared in the sky as the constellation Coma Berenice, Berenice's Hair. One of the stars is named Al Ḍafīrah, "the curl."

* * *

The Wafiomi said a woman must not cut her hair for one year after her first menstruation. Before marriage, a Hopi woman wore a whorled, squash-blossom hairstyle resembling butterfly wings on either side of her head. After marriage, she braided her hair in a single plait. The Spartans said that before the wedding a bride must cut her hair short, wear the cloak and sandals of a man, and lie alone on a pallet in the dark. The Romans parted a bride's hair with a *hasta recurva*, or bent spear hook, and this was called "combing the hair of the virgin." The Turks said a bride should weave her hair into twenty to thirty braids twined with silver tinsel and attach a blue bead at the end of one to ward off the evil eye. "The hairs are Cupid's nets, to catch all comers," Robert Burton noted in *The Anatomy of Melancholy*. The Ilocano said a pregnant woman should refrain from leaving the house at night with her hair let down so as not to give birth to a snake. The Hindus said a man should part the hair of his pregnant wife three times from front to back to ensure the proper development of the embryo. In Oldenburg, women wrapped clippings of their hair and nails in a cloth and placed the cloth beneath a tree three days before the new moon as a cure for infertility. In Punjab, a woman who washed her hair and threw the dirty water over an infant in order to kill him and capture his spirit for her womb was known as *gille val*, a wet hair. Egyptian women buried a lock of their hair with their deceased husband as a charm of protection in the afterlife. In Mexico, women kept their hair combings in special jars, which were buried with them when they died, so their souls would not look for the loose strands and postpone passage to the other world. Victorian women wore brooches made with the hair of their deceased loved ones. Yoko Ono cut her hair after the murder of her husband, saying, "John loved my long hair, so I gave it to him." A clipping of Princess Diana's hair sold for ten dollars on eBay.

* * *

"But if a woman has long hair," the apostle Paul wrote in his letter to the Corinthians, "it is a glory to her." God wished women to rejoice in their locks "as a horse in his mane," said Clement of Alexandria. A sixth-century commentary on the book of Genesis urged all women to cover their heads, "like one who commits a crime and is abashed by it." Kimhit, as noted in the Talmud, bore seven sons who became high priests, and attributed her good fortune to the fact that even the beams of her house had never seen a lock of her hair. "If you despoil the most outstandingly beautiful woman of her hair . . . were she Venus herself . . . she would not be able to seduce even her own husband," said Apuleius. The Iranians punished an adulteress by cutting off her braid, referring to her thereafter as a "cut braid." "If a woman reveals her hair on her head she causes a different kind of hair to be revealed," Rabbi Judah said. For every strand of hair that a woman exposes she will burn a day in hell, the Muslims said. Churchmen declared Joan of Arc apostate for cutting off her hair, and set a miter-shaped paper cap on her head inscribed with the words *heretic*, *relapsed*, *apostate*, *idolatress*. A slave, raped by her master, had her hair cut off as punishment by his wife. A slave master, angry about a slave's pregnancy, took a pair of shears to her head. "Long hair, short intelligence," said the Turks. In Cuba, María Hernández fled to the Marianao police station because her husband vowed to beat her to death after she cut her hair. "Bobbed Hair Leads to Suit for Divorce." "Shocked Husband Shoots Himself when Wife Bobs Her Hair." "Girl Bobs Hair, Mourns Tresses, Jumps in River." "Mussolini Now Wars on Bobbed Hair." "Does Bobbed Hair Interfere with the Efficiency of the Student Nurse?" "Bobbed hair is a state of mind," said opera singer Mary Garden, "and not merely a manner of dressing my hair." Frenchwomen accused of "horizontal collaboration" with the Nazis were subject to public head shaving. A secretary in New York, her hair shaved off by a jealous wife, was awarded $117,500 in damages. "Hair is women's life," according to a Japanese proverb.

* * *

Antigone boasted her hair was prettier than Hera's, and for this she was turned into a stork. The poet Menander said that a woman with dyed yellow hair was unchaste and a lazy housekeeper. The Romans sheared the blond hair off German slaves to make into wigs. Cyprian, bishop of Carthage, said that a woman who wore false hair committed a sin more grievous than adultery. Madame Lauzun's favorite hairstyle was a headdress of natural and artificial hair, topped by ducks swimming in the sea, next to scenes of hunting and shooting, held together by beef marrow and stuffed with wool, tow, and hemp. A sixteenth-century history of witchcraft maintained that women with yellow hair were more frequently visited by incubi. To honor the king's smallpox inoculation, Marie Antoinette's hairdresser created the *pouf a l'inoculation*, featuring a rising sun and an olive tree with a serpent entwined around its trunk. German women drank beer and cider to increase the crop of their hair for harvest. The Seven Sutherland Sisters, who toured with Barnum and Bailey, had the Longest Hair in the World, a combined thirty-six feet, ten inches. Former slave Lucy Key used a hairbrush called a "Jim Crow" that "mortally took skin, hair, and all." The Nazis sent the shorn hair of Jewish women to Bavaria for the manufacture of felt. Marilyn Monroe used a shade of hair dye called Dirty Pillow Slip. Alfred Hitchcock said, "Blondes are the best victims. They're like virgin snow which shows up the bloody footprints." Manibhen Yashwanthpur prayed to the Hindu god Lord Venkateswara for her husband to stop beating her, and later, when he desisted for a month, she went to the temple in thanks and offered her hair as a sacrifice. The impoverished wife of a Burmese political prisoner sold her hair for the equivalent of twenty dollars. My mother, voiceless and dying of thyroid cancer, wrote a note before treatment saying, *They are going to wrap my head in cold ice packs to help preserve the hair.*

PART TWO

Leopold and Shinner

ONE

June 2, 1957: "Should Leopold Be Paroled?"

The *Chicago Sunday Tribune* wanted your opinion. So did Nathan Leopold. Leopold, who, along with Richard Loeb, murdered Bobby Franks in 1924. The crime was dubbed a "thrill kill," murder for kicks, "the crime of the century." Leopold and Loeb: young, smart, wealthy, educated, Jewish, homosexual. At the time of the murder, they were, respectively, nineteen and eighteen years old, students at the University of Chicago, and lovers. Loeb was killed in prison in 1936. Now, after thirty-three years, Nathan Leopold would soon be up for parole. "Expiation? Atonement? Whether I have paid my debt to society? . . . Other people will have to decide."

Other people did. Erle Stanley Gardner, creator of the Perry Mason detective series and author of the introduction to Leopold's prison memoir, *Life Plus 99 Years*, wrote, "Here is a man who [is trying to] live down the tragic mistake of his youth. . . . Will society meet him halfway?" Carl Sandburg invited him to his home. *Chicago Sun-Times* columnist Irv "Kup" Kupcinet expressed confidence that he would make an "exemplary parolee." And, noting that his support was not limited to people of influence, Leopold said, "Little John Smith and Mrs. Mary Jones . . . are writing me every day."

My mother was one of the Mrs. Mary Joneses. Harriet Shinner, née Alter. She wrote a letter in support of Leopold's parole. She was thirty-three, married with two children, ages six and two. Paying monthly mortgage payments on a two-bedroom brick ranch in Peterson Park on the Northwest Side of Chicago. She wore housecoats, monitored her weight, smoked Marlboros, played mah-jongg. Worried about money. Read popular novels (*Peyton Place* made the *New York Times* best seller list for fifty-nine weeks in 1956–57). She had fair skin, a sharp nose, sorrowful eyes. She was easily hurt. Born in 1924, the same year as the murder; Jewish, like both the victim and the perpetrators (although Loeb's mother was Catholic and therefore, according to Jewish law, not Jewish); and her husband's name, my father's, was also Nathan. As far as I know, she wasn't particularly civic minded, she wasn't a member of the League of Women Voters or a volunteer at a soup kitchen; nor did she write letters to the editor about local ordinances, like some women did. She wasn't that kind of woman. Nor was she, as far as I know, the kind of woman who would watch the House Committee on Un-American Activities hearings during the summer of 1951, while she was pregnant with me, but, as she later told me, she did.

* * *

I know that my mother wrote to Nathan Leopold because I have the letter that Leopold wrote to her. It's addressed to Mrs. Nathan Shinner, a common erasure of self my mother subscribed to, I suspect, without hesitation. *When I was at Stateville, making every effort to win my release, I promised myself that, once freed, I would send personal replies to all who wrote me. In prison I was restricted in ways that made general correspondence impossible, and I longed for the time when I might show my gratitude to all who were friendly enough to write a stranger. It has taken a long time, I fear, to get around to this letter, but finally the day has come.* Finally the day has come. Did she await his letter with as much anticipation as he apparently felt before he wrote it? The letter is postmarked Puerto Rico—where Leopold went to work as a medical technician—and stamped with a soaring airplane, whose skyward trajectory seems to highlight the eager flight toward its destination. Postage was seven cents; the name of the return addressee simply N L. The raised punch of the typewritten letters, pounded, it appears, with steady force, comes through to the back of the envelope.

* * *

I found the letter in a drawer in the hutch in our dining room when I was snooping around for secrets. It was an idle kind of snooping, a listless looking around, propelled by a subterranean, undirected energy. I did it often, starting at ten, eleven years old, when my parents were out with their monthly couples' club, and I turned to my weekend amusement. Going through the nightstand, the dresser, my mother's old floral jewelry bag, coming across some old, long-forgotten scarf, heavy with the odor of makeup and musty perfume, or a smutty birthday gift someone had given my father, a mock trophy for his putter. Once, from these drawers, my mother had taken out a condom and filled it with water, to show me what it would look like stretched over something, and I remember being embarrassed by the word *engorged*. And after my father died, when I was thirty-seven years old and newly orphaned—a status that simultaneously throws you back into being a child and confers upon you the mantle of irrevocable adulthood—I emptied the drawers, whatever was to be dug up now part of my rightful inheritance, and found a manila envelope labeled *For Peggy Only*. Inside was one of my short stories, cut up, the lesbian references excised, and the remaining sections taped back together, so, I surmised, he could be the proud father (but not too proud) and show my work to his lady friend, Rose. On the one hand I was stunned that he felt he had the right to undertake such wholesale hacking, and on the other amused by the care he took, not to hide his actions but to leave me the record.

Did I expect to get the goods on my parents during these nosings? A part of me was looking for excitement, something that would put our lives up on the marquee or at least toss them in the air and set them back down in a slightly different arrangement. As a child I had chafed against the navy-blue hooded hat my mother made me wear in winter, with holes for the eyes, nose, and mouth, a hat that seemed to close off everything. *Please don't let me be like my mother*, I prayed years later lying in bed as a teenager, unsure about the ethical legitimacy of a plea to God when I'd never before shown my allegiance, but sure, in my hyperinflated angst, about its meaning: *Don't let me lead a life so confined*.

We kept a few dusty bottles of liquor in the hutch, and the china (which I've since inherited and given away to the resale shop), and some random pieces of little-used glassware. In one of the drawers was a set of specialty knives, each in its own cushioned bed. I don't remember when I found the letter or if my mother was alive or not, but if she was alive I do know I never asked her about it. I don't remember if I even knew who Nathan Leopold was. (My brother says he remembers talking to her about the letter, or thinks he remembers, and part of me doesn't believe him, as if he's lying—not intentionally, but because he doesn't want to miss his chance at a piece of history. But I don't want to miss out either, which is why another part of me is jealous he has a memory I don't, even if it's a memory he hardly remembers.) The envelope, a #10, had been slit across the top, and I can picture her long-nailed finger running under the sealed edge.

TWO

After my father died, I took the letter home with me and put it in another drawer. Occasionally I would take it out and read it, as if it were written in code and all I had to do was crack it; as if scanning the punched-out letters would tell me something about my mother. Occasionally I would parade it before friends like a trophy, something that I'd earned and would speak well of me. *I have a letter from Nathan Leopold*, I'd announce, waiting to see if they were impressed, and feeling deflated and a little embarrassed if I saw a flicker of incomprehension, forcing me to ask, politely and in apology, *Do you know who he is?* I felt vaguely ashamed at my quest for cheap celebrity.

The letter was an artifact, like her wallet, wristwatch, keychain, social security card, also put away in a drawer; a memento of my mother. But lately it feels as though I can hardly remember her. I was twenty-nine when she died; I've lived over half my life without her. She defended me against the bullies in my neighborhood, stayed up all night painting a Chicago flag for my fourth-grade social studies project, and, my arm held aloft in the air with hers, taught me to dance the box step across the kitchen floor. Leopold's letter was one side of the equation. What about the other? I didn't know how much I wanted to find her letter—like a missing piece of evidence, which assumes more importance the longer you look—until I searched through the archives at Northwestern University, home to a collection of Leopold and Loeb materials, and it didn't turn up.

THREE

I don't think my mother would have used a typewriter. I don't think we owned one then. We didn't get one until I was in high school.

She would have written her letter by hand. I always admired her handwriting, because it looked so sophisticated: sleek, lean, no baby fat. *Compulsion*, she wrote on the outside of Nathan Leopold's letter in blue ballpoint, *Meyer Levin*, perhaps a reminder to herself to get Levin's 1956 fictionalized account of the murder and read it, which, if I had to guess, and I do, I'd say that she did.

* * *

They wrote to him from all over: Indianapolis, Indiana; Amityville, New York; Tampa, Florida; Uniontown, Pennsylvania; Iron Mountain, Michigan; Ponchatoula, Louisiana; Aberdeen, South Dakota; Beloit, Wisconsin; Chatfield, Minnesota; Houston, Texas; Waurika, Oklahoma; Witbank, South Africa; Stollings, West Virginia; North Hollywood, California; Washington, DC; Spokane, Washington; Portland, Maine; Saluda, North Carolina; Webster Groves, Missouri; Fort Lyons, Colorado; Toronto, Canada; Middletown, Ohio; Brandon, Vermont; Woonsocket, Rhode Island; Louisville, Kentucky; Hanover, Germany; Butte, Montana; McComb, Mississippi; Portland, Oregon; Manchester, New Hampshire; Baltimore, Maryland; Greenwich, Connecticut; South Orange, New Jersey; Lichtervelde, Belgium; Boston, Massachusetts; Spartanburg, South Carolina; Alexandria, Virginia; Cookeville, Tennessee.

* * *

She wrote to him from the kitchen table. Perhaps my father was working late at the laundromat, counting quarters. The dishes were washed, the children finally in bed. She had a cigarette going in the ashtray; the tip was rimmed in red. *Nathan Leopold. Stateville Prison. Joliet, Illinois.* How did she begin? I combed the records at Northwestern. How did *they* begin? Little John Smith, Mrs. Mary Jones. I made copies of their letters in the files. Some were formal, some intimate; some immediately chatty. Some sounded like they were the best of friends. Dear Mr. Leopold; My dear Sir; Dear Nathan; Dear Leopold; Good morning Nate; My dear Nathan; Dear Sir; Dear Nate; Dear Nat; Dear friend; Nathan Leopold; My Dear; Dearest Nathan; Our Dear Friend.

* * *

He wrote to her from Castañer, a village sixty-five miles southwest of San Juan, in the highlands of Puerto Rico, at an altitude of four thousand feet. The Church of the Brethren, headquartered outside Chicago, ran a mission hospital there. He took x-rays for ten dollars a week, plus room and board. *I am very happy here at Castañer. The members of the Project are as dedicated a group of men and women as could be found anywhere in the world. They have been kindness itself in their treatment of me. My work in the hospital laboratory and pharmacy is very interesting and keeps me very busy. My evenings I have been devoting to writing letters.*

FOUR

The facts were never in dispute. Ten days after kidnapping Bobby Franks, fatally striking him in the head with a chisel, pouring hydrochloric acid over his face and genitals after he was dead to hinder identification, stuffing his naked body into a culvert, and trying to extort a ten-thousand-dollar ransom from his family, Nathan Leopold and Richard Loeb confessed to the killing. The motive was the question. Why had they murdered fourteen-year-old Franks, a randomly chosen victim? Leopold, a geeky, self-described Nietzschean, put it this way during the police investigation: "The thing that prompted Dick . . . and . . . me to want to do this . . . was a sort of pure love of excitement, or the imaginary love of thrills, doing something different . . . the satisfaction and ego of putting something over." Smart boys, they wanted to outsmart all comers.

Cook County state's attorney Robert Crowe didn't buy it. Thrills, he sneered. They didn't do it for thrills. "Not the thrill and the delight and the fast beating heart that they [the defense, i.e. Clarence Darrow] tell you Dickie Loeb has, if he has got a heart at all." No. "All through this case it is money, money, money." (The *Chicago Tribune* estimated the combined assets of the Leopold and Loeb families at somewhere between 15 million and 25 million dollars and, linking them to other rich Chicago Jewish families, referred to the "Jewish '400.'") Money was the motive, Crowe asserted, even though they already had plenty. Money and perversion. They were perverts, he said. Degenerates. (Meaning homosexual and Jewish, two attributes often conflated into one. "Show me a Jew and you show me a Uranian [male homosexual]," wrote American writer Edward Stevenson in his 1908 history of homosexuality, echoing a crude statement then in currency. Later, Hitler would maintain that homosexuality was caused by "Jewish blood.") They committed perversions on each other. Didn't Nathan Leopold admit to fantasies of raping a child? Wasn't he planning to gallivant around "Paris or some other of the gay capitals of Europe, indulging his unnatural lust with the $5,000 he had wrung from Jacob Franks [Bobby Franks's father]"? Didn't the coroner's report on Bobby Franks say that "the rectum was dilated, [and] would easily admit one finger"? (The report also indicated there was "no evidence of a recent forcible dilation," but Crowe chose to ignore that.)

Darrow said there was no motive. The crime was "senseless, useless, purposeless, motiveless." This was the act of two boys who were mentally ill (throughout the hearing, Darrow repeatedly called them boys or children, or referred to them in the diminutive, Dickie Loeb and Babe [his nickname] Leopold, to underscore their youth and lack of emotional maturity and to elicit sympathy). A human being, according to Darrow, was like an apparatus; it either worked, or it didn't. "Is Dickie Loeb to blame because . . . he was born without [emotional capacity]? . . . Is he to blame that his machine is imperfect?" Nathan, he argued, was "just half a boy, an intellect, an intellectual machine going without . . . a governor." (When it came to crime, Richard and Nathan weren't nearly so smart as they had thought. They left behind a trail of evidence, the most incriminating being Nathan's glasses, dropped at the forest preserve where they dumped Franks's body. If you hire one boy to do a job, an old proverb goes, you've got a whole boy. Hire two boys, and you've got half a boy. Hire three, and you've got no boy at all.)

FIVE

Take a look at them, the medical specialists said in the sensational days leading up to the trial. The papers ran head shots. Phrenological diagrams of their faces in profile. (Phrenology, the study of personality based on the size of specific brain areas.) The crime, writ upon the body. It's all there: murderer, Jew, queer. The curve of Leopold's skull, indicating he's lacking in moral qualities, reasoning, and benevolence. The protruding sex center, located in the cerebellum, showing that "his sex feelings predominate." His large nose, suggestive of aggressiveness; sensuous lips; the cartilaginous fold within the rim of the ear, similar to that of Aaron Burr, third vice president of the United States and killer of Alexander Hamilton in the notorious duel, indicating a "dynamic" personality.

As for Loeb: He is "the female type." "His mouth turns up in the curve of vanity." He too has sensuous lips. His prominent chin suggests a love of excitement, leading to loss of control. His skull shows that he's secretive and a liar. Dr. James M. Fitzgerald, "expert in character analysis," noted phrenologist of thirty-five years, compared their photos. Both boys, he concluded, venturing beyond his phrenological expertise to tie it all together, have always "had their needs anticipated. They have never had to earn a penny, only knew how to throw away a dollar. . . . There was no moral check. They were surfeited with books, elegance, ultra-refinement. They led an upholstered life."

* * *

Degenerates, State's Attorney Crowe called them. Drawing on the theory of degeneration promulgated across Europe in the mid- to late nineteenth century by various doctors, criminologists, forensic scientists, and literati, among them writer Émile Zola. (We had on our bookshelf at home a green leather-bound copy of Zola's *Nana*, an anomaly among the drugstore best sellers my mother usually read.) According to French psychiatrist Bénédict Augustin Morel, degenerations were "deviations from the normal human type . . . transmissible by heredity and . . . deteriorat[ing] progressively toward extinction." Italian criminologist Cesare Lombroso said degenerates had certain defining characteristics, dubbed the "stigmata of degeneration": enormous jaws, sloping foreheads, high cheekbones, large chins, hawk-like noses, bulging eyes (a 1957 *Chicago Tribune* article described Leopold's eyes as "large, protruding, and often filled with tears"). Going even further, Dr. Ambroise Tardieu claimed the pederast (synonymous with *homosexual*, whom he also called "auntie") had an underdeveloped, tapered penis, like that of a dog: underdeveloped, suggesting less masculine, yet tapered and so the better to penetrate its victim. In a different but related context—fin-de-siècle Vienna—where anti-Semitism and homophobia came together in a salacious and not altogether unfunny mix, the slang for *clitoris* was the "Jew," referring to the circumcised, that is, truncated, penis. Female masturbation was "playing with the Jew."

* * *

(Phrenology, even in its nineteenth-century heyday decried by some as a pseudoscience, suffered a blow when an autopsy revealed that Franz Josef Gall, one of its leading proponents, had a brain that weighed "a meager 1,198 grams." [Brain weighing was somewhat the rage among nineteenth-century craniometricians, according to paleontologist Stephen Jay Gould. The "European average," Gould notes, was 1,300 to 1,400 grams.])

SIX

Professional do-gooders, sob sisters, pseudoscientists. That's what a Cook County assistant state's attorney called supporters of Leopold's parole at a 1953 hearing.

After over thirty years in the pen, he was diminished. A journalist, the same one who queried, "Should Leopold Be Paroled?" described him as a humble man with halting speech who now took fifty units of insulin a day for his diabetes. In his prison garb—jeans and a denim shirt with his inmate number, 9306D, on the back—he hovered like "a pudgy shadow."

No longer arrogant and cocksure, Leopold seemed stumped by what he'd done. He couldn't understand it. Nor, as he was frisked an average of sixteen times per day, could he forget it. His lover Loeb was long dead. His father too. His favorite aunt. His older brother, who, without fail, had come every two weeks to visit. *Forsan et haec olim meminisse iuvabit*; he'd affixed the words from Virgil's *Aeneid* on the wall of his cell at Stateville. *Perhaps one day this will be worth remembering.* Trying to explain his behavior to the parole board four years earlier, in 1953, he'd attributed it to immaturity, stupidity. "I couldn't give a motive which makes sense to me. It was the act of a child," he said, "a simpleton kid. A very bizarre act. I don't know why I did it. I'm a different man now," he said, seemingly helpless in the face of whatever man he was.

* * *

Sob sister: denoting a female journalist who wrote sentimental stories or an actress who played "pathetic roles"; any sentimental, impractical woman. The term originated in 1907 at another infamous trial, that of millionaire Harry Kendall Thaw for the murder of architect Stanford White, where the four female journalists who covered the case, according to one source, "spread their sympathy like jam."

SEVEN

Dear Mr. Leopold,

Some surprised themselves by writing. They didn't know why they did it. They'd never written a stranger before. They were disconcerted by their actions. Almost apologetic. "I don't make a practice of writing to strangers . . ." "This is not a run-of the- mill letter." "My biography['s] in *Who's Who*." As if a recitation of credentials could separate them from the ordinary pack of supporters, supplicants, and mawkish voyeurs. Some had read excerpts of his autobiography in the *Chicago Daily News*. "I can truthfully say I've done more thinking about you in the past few months than any other alive and breathing individual." "I can't help but wonder if you are the person I think you to be, the one I've come to know." They talked to their mothers about him. Their spouses. Their friends. "Last week my mother and I were speaking about your case and she said 'and now he is sorry for all he has done to his loved ones and he lights yortsite [*sic*] . . . candles for them' and with this she began to cry—not for you, but for herself." Perhaps a man who had spent over 60 percent of his life in prison cast an uncanny light on their own fading dreams.

* * *

My mother and I never spoke about his case. We never talked about him. I don't know if she was in the habit of writing to strangers or if she too professed this was her first time. I don't know what impulse, sentiment, conviction, or opinion prompted her to write to him. Was she, as the assistant state's attorney accused of others, a sob sister? A sentimental, impractical woman? I know she was shy.

Diffident. But she also had a streak of impetuousness. She could be smitten. Consider this: she met my father at a downtown kiosk, where he sold sundries and ran a little bookie operation (a minor mob man), asked him to light her cigarette, and three months later shed her name and took up his. She was sophisticated, well dressed, savvy; twenty-four years old, fashionably but not desperately older than the median marrying age in 1948 (20.4, according to the US Bureau of the Census), and working in a downtown dress house. I love this version of my mother, with its glamour and daring, but it's not the only one. Consider this too: after they got married, she persuaded my father to give it up, to go legit. She didn't want to be a mob moll. He sold the kiosk and they bought a laundromat, where they washed, dried, and folded other people's clothes.

* * *

Some were religious. They wanted Leopold to welcome Jesus into his heart. With Jesus as his constant companion, the path would be clear, the road smooth. All would be forgiven. We have all sinned. Who among us has not sinned? "*You* are the one who can say 'and now I have changed' which is what everyone of us is seeking—and by your example we are each strengthened in our own struggle." Some acknowledged that he worshiped another God, but then said Jesus was a Jew too. "In Revelations the New Testament, there will be 144,000 Jews saved. Now I invite you to be one of the number and come into this fold." Some said they would pray for him, he was in their prayers. "I've just mailed a letter to The Boss, special Delivery, for He has the power to pivot someone your way to toss you a key," presumably to release and redemption.

* * *

Did she write to him because he was Jewish? Did she experience a fellow feeling? Was she standing up for one of her own? Even though Leopold was from a well-heeled family of German Jews who'd made their fortune in shipping and the manufacture of aluminum cans and paper boxes and my mother was the daughter of a Russian immigrant sign painter not long removed from the shtetl, they were on the same team. Jews don't commit crimes, according to the old saw given quintessential voice by Jewish writer Harold Berman in a 1924 issue of the *Open Court*: "The very thought of looking for Jewish names in the ranks of the professional rowdy and the criminal ... was as ludicrous as ... Antediluvian monsters stalking the sidewalks of Twentieth Century Broadway." (Berman admitted, however, that by the 1920s there had been an "outbreak of gangsterism in New York's [Jewish] Ghetto.") An outdated hyperbole, but one, I suspect, my mother believed in as well. Did Leopold's Jewishness exonerate him? Make him, if not less guilty, more redeemable? Was she more likely to forgive a Jew, because a Jew wasn't a real criminal? (Or was he not a "real" Jew? That's what some leaders in the Jewish community claimed about both Leopold and Loeb in 1924. Their families had lost their way as Jews, had been too concerned with wealth and money. "The truth is that these two Jewish boys were not under the influence of Judaism, and they are not Jewish products," Dr. S. M. Melamed, editor of the *Jewish Courier*, maintained.)

Perhaps she was swayed by popular columnist Irv Kupcinet, a darling of the Jewish community, who advocated on Leopold's behalf. He was from the same North Lawndale neighborhood as she, the same Russian immigrant background. She read his column faithfully. He made reference to Leopold's petition for parole several times before the board's decision in early 1958. Restating the "Lincoln-like" words of Carl Sandburg, Kup said, "The world will little remember if you turn down Leopold; but you will not be forgotten if you grant him freedom."

* * *

Some offered advice. Don't look back, they said. Square your shoulders, lift your chin. You're not that boy anymore. Study law. Go to work for the State Department. Put all the butter you want on a roll. Study Mr. Goren's (world champion bridge master) ideas about bridge. Write about the Midwest countryside. "How the fields go on and on, each more beautifully fertile than the one before . . ." Go to Israel. "You would be a great asset to that new little country," someone from Louisiana said.

Others offered friendship. Conversation. Coffee and a snack. Stop by sometime. "My phone number is . . ." "I make good coffee." We'll talk about language, poetry, prose, music, art, government, birds. "We call the house 'Rose-Star!' and have many wonderful philosophical sessions around the kitchen table." Do you like cats? Here's a picture of Chop Chop when he was three months old. He has a delightful personality. Come to California. "I would love to point out some of its sites to you personally." Come to Aberdeen. It's got some of the best duck, pheasant, and goose hunting around. The holidays are coming. "I . . . bought you a few things for Passover and hope they reach you in time. . . . I'd hate to think you didn't have a slab of matzes [*sic*] to get constipated on," one woman joked.

Let me introduce myself, some said. Height. Weight. Hair. Eyes. Age. Vital statistics. Family lineage. "I am Irish and Italian with a soupçon of Amsterdam Dutch thrown in." "Lived part of my young life in Kentucky So you see I am a Southerer [*sic*]." A catalogue of likes and dislikes. Love books, poetry, flowers, water, houses, shoes, copper luster pitchers. Hate canaries, cards, diamonds, liver, people without humility. Slings and arrows. "My Daughter says I talk to much [*sic*]. Her father said I didn't talk enough." "I was engaged to [Hirschel Rivkin] until his [parents] discovered I went to the CATHOLIC CHURCH. . . . You look like him."

* * *

Some professed love. Longing. They were used to their loneliness, or so they'd thought; they'd filled their lives with business, clubs, teaching, but then out of the blue he came along. Write to me, they said. Visit me. Settle nearby. "You'd laugh if you had seen me looking at your picture through my magnifying glass." Here's a copy of Kipling's poem "If." "I wouldn't give it to anyone but you." "You're a Kipling kind of 'man.'" "I love every hair on your head." When he didn't return their affections, they were aggrieved. How could you go so far away to Puerto Rico? "It hurts" that you don't answer. Perhaps you'll find "I'm too fat." Still, they said, it's better to love someone with your whole heart—someone who doesn't even know you—than never to have found "the one" at all.

And if it wasn't actually love they offered, how about a more pragmatic ardor? A mutually beneficial arrangement? "If you should decide on the book store job in Chicago, I am Laura Mae, I want to marry you."

* * *

Some wanted a piece of history, of something larger and more enduring than themselves. Give me your autograph, they said. Enclosed is a stamped, self-addressed envelope. Sign here. (Leopold himself wrote to Albert Einstein on the pretense of wanting to study relativity. But, as he eventually admitted, "I had a desire to own a letter of his." Essayist Anne Fadiman, a polar enthusiast, bought a letter by explorer Robert Falcon Scott because "it was something I believed I could not live without." And I, of course, have Leopold's letter, the value of which seemed to me negligible [in monetary terms], or at least strictly personal, until I thought of donating it to the Northwestern University archive, and then, suddenly, I didn't want to give it up.)

Others had more material interests. They wanted to strike a deal. Write an essay, one man suggested, "especially for me." Title it "When I'm Free." On the day of your release, "I would sell the article to the highest bidder among newspapers. . . . It would tend to soften antagonists [*sic*] reaction to [you] . . . and would make me some money, so I could continue my writing more comfortably."

EIGHT

Did she know that Nathan Leopold was gay? That he and Richard Loeb had been lovers? Much was made of their relationship at the time of the trial. "Loeb 'Master' of Leopold under Solemn Pact Made," a headline in the *Chicago Daily Tribune* read. According to psychiatrists for the defense, the two teens had come to an agreement months prior to the killing: Leopold would participate in Loeb's criminal escapades (which stemmed from an initial fascination with detective magazines, and were later amplified and distorted by his contemptuous disregard for societal constraints) in exchange for sex three times every two months. Leopold was "abject . . . [in his] devotion to Loeb, saying that he was jealous of the food and drink that Loeb took." The pact sealed a bond founded on a complex mix of dependence, desire, and criminal pathology.

The depth of this connection was acutely evident in Leopold's account of Richard Loeb's death. In 1936, Loeb was slashed fifty-six times by a fellow prisoner who claimed he was the target of sexual assault, a charge that was never substantiated.

Nathan Leopold rushed to the prison hospital to be by Loeb's side. He stood at the foot of the bed as the doctors failed to stanch the flow of blood from Loeb's neck. Then, he tended to the body. He washed Loeb's wounds; helped sew up the cuts, still bleeding, on his back. "Cut to ribbons," he notes in his memoir. Covering Loeb with a sheet, he put the body to rest, but a moment later pulled the cover back. "I wanted a long last look at him." Then he sat on a stool next to the operating table until hospital officials took Richard Loeb away.

In the 1950s, when Leopold was up for parole and my mother, presumably, was following the case, the papers once again carried various references, coded and not, to their relationship. Loeb: his infatuation. Loeb: a juvenile affair. Loeb: his pal. Loeb: his friend. Loeb: "his best friend but his worst enemy." Loeb: "I admired [him] extravagantly," Leopold said. "Loeb, under whose influence he was [*sic*]." "I would have done anything he asked," Leopold admitted. "I lived and died [for] his approval and disapproval."

And would she, Harriet Shinner, née Alter, have approved or disapproved? I don't know how she would have parsed it out. She might have avoided the subject altogether, preferring not to consider such things. After all, Nathan Leopold himself, with his freedom in the balance, declared that he was washed clean. All signs of homosexuality obliterated. "I have changed completely," he told the parole board. "My personality, even my physical being has changed. *No cell that was in my body at the time of the crime is there today*" (emphasis mine). Implying that all aberrant impulses, homosexuality included, which lodge at the very deepest, that is, the cellular level, had, through the scouring action of time and contrition, been flushed from his body. Speaking before the parole board in 1958, Leopold's attorney Elmer Gertz made a similar point: "The prison records will bear out, and the public should know it, that there is not the slightest evidence of sexual impropriety." Several years later, however, when he visited Leopold's apartment in Puerto Rico, Gertz was discomfited to find a photo of himself on the wall next to one of Richard Loeb.

But when I was coming out in the mid-1970s, my mother's disapproval was perfectly clear. You always side with them, she said, when, to get her goat, I'd made an aggressively positive comment about a gay man standing outside a hair salon near Michigan Avenue. I'd wanted to provoke her anger on the one hand *and* force her to stand up for me on the other. Her accusation automatically gave rise to a line in the sand. I was one of *them*.

Can't you at least try it with a man? she pleaded on another occasion, improbably exhorting me to engage in heterosexual sex in the hope that the overwhelming nature of the experience would convert me. And when I did not carry through with her plea? She's so mannish, my mother said about my partner, Ann.

Finally, in the months before her death from thyroid cancer, my mother suggested that her illness was a response to my lesbianism, as if lesbianism could have somehow breached the boundaries of my body and caused her cells to errantly multiply and go awry. A lump lodged in her throat; she could no longer swallow, lesbianism or anything else.

NINE

What did my mother offer? What, if anything, did she serve up? I doubt she told Leopold that she'd always wanted a nose job or that she'd had braces when she was twenty years old. Nor did she tell him it was difficult to communicate with my sometimes argumentative father—something, I suspect, she didn't even tell herself until years later, when she gave way to bouts of anger and despair. Her own mother, with her drafts and chills and Sarah Bernhardt histrionics, was driving her crazy. No, she didn't tell him that. Her first pregnancy resulted in miscarriage, a clot of blood in the toilet. Not that either. Did she tell him that when she was a child perilously ill with appendicitis, her parents went to the synagogue, and for a penny warded off the evil eye and staved off death?

That she sat and stared out the living room window past the heart-shaped leaves of the catalpa? That she encouraged me to be brainy and self-reliant but instead I turned bookish and aloof? That she said I was a cold fish? *I'll never forget this for as long as I live,* she said once, but refused to tell me what it was. *If you don't know,* she said, *I can't tell you.* But all this, of course, was much later.

I doubt she told him anything other than what the hundreds of other Little John Smiths and Mrs. Mary Joneses politely and sincerely told him: that he'd paid his dues; atoned for his crime; been rehabilitated. He deserved a chance.

Yours truly, Mrs. Nathan Shinner.

* * *

And if she offered him a chance, what did he offer her? A secret life, a life nobody knew about, far from the sleeping children and the whir of other people's clothes spinning in the dryer? The House Committee on Un-American Activities. Leopold. The view out the living room window. Perhaps that's what she wanted. If not another life, a glimpse at one. One that she slipped into the drawer in the hutch and kept hidden from all of us. (Now my California-dwelling brother has the hutch; inert and battered, it sits like an old ship run aground in his dining room. When I visited recently, it took me a moment to recognize it.) Because why am I convinced that she never told my father, that one Nathan didn't know about the other? I want her to have her secret. I want to give her that life.

* * *

Months later Leopold responded. November 19, 1958.

The country-side is unbelievably beautiful. Here we are in a little valley, completely surrounded by mountain green all year round. Flowers and birds are here in profusion; there is actually a gardenia bush, which seems to bloom all the time, just outside my door.

The Puerto Ricans have been very good to me. They have accepted me without too much curiosity and many of them have expressed themselves as pleased that I have chosen this beautiful island as my home.

Certainly everything necessary seems to be at hand to give me the opportunity of doing useful work. I will certainly do my best. I hope very much that I can justify your faith and that of my many other friends in me. . . .

Please accept my heartfelt gratitude. . . . I will never forget you.

Sincerely yours, Nathan F. Leopold Jr.

TEN

At first I was confident I would find her letter in the files. They were marked *Letters supporting N. Leopold parole. N. Leopold correspondence received. Fan letters to N. Leopold* (as if his notoriety had granted him celebrity status or transformed him into a commodity, and now he was a Hall of Fame athlete or a favorite brand of soap). *September 1957. October 1957. February 1958. S—. March 1958. S–Z.* There were so many letters. Was my mother a fan? Each was stamped CENSORED, with a number underneath. CENSORED/20, the number perhaps a code for the prison official who opened the letter and read it. Each envelope neatly slit. One letter was addressed *Mr. Nathan Loeb*, Leopold's first name, Richard's last—an understandable confusion, as their names had, in the sensational aftermath of the killing, melded into one long name, one murdering monolith, LeopoldandLoeb; and now, over thirty years later, this new amalgam, a supercriminal, half of each of them, Mr. Nathan Loeb. RETURN TO SENDER, the envelope was stamped. (Did Nathan Leopold ever see this letter? Did he rail at the sender's sloppiness, or did one small part of him welcome being reunited with his long-deceased lover in this patchwork way?) NOT. HERE. someone had written, which felt at the same time odd and dismissive: Nathan Loeb was never here.

I looked for the stylish slant of her handwriting (which I pictured in blue, probably because the *Compulsion* she wrote on the back of Leopold's envelope was in blue), our return address, which was the address of the Bernard Street house where I grew up and wrote my name in chalk on the bricks. I searched calmly enough at first, but then I grew restless and disappointed. It was as if I were looking for her, a piece of her, pawing through piles of rubble, mounds of envelopes and stationery and greeting cards (*time you were OUT . . . AND ABOUT!*) with peeling six-cent postage stamps and rubber-stamped cancellations. Digging for remains. The letter had become transformed: not a letter she had written to Nathan Leopold but one written to me, and in it she would cede part of herself, some part that, up until now, had been concealed, and then, through these scavenged words, we would be reunited, like Leopold and Loeb were reunited through Mr. Nathan Loeb.

So many letters, but none hers. I was exhausted by the effort of reading them. I couldn't shake the feeling I'd been stood up. I'd arrived at the assigned destination, but my date didn't deign to come. Had I been found wanting? I felt exposed. Nor could I shake the feeling I was insufficiently devoted. I was not one of those relatives who, in search of new evidence, exhumed the body after all. At some point I stopped looking. Instead, I scraped together whatever fragments I could, paid five cents a copy for other people's letters, stapled, sorted, and labeled them, and put them in a file of my own. Nathan Leopold's letter to Mrs. Nathan Shinner sits on top of them all.

ELEVEN

The letter Nathan Leopold wrote my mother was not meant specially for her. It was meant for every Little John Smith and Mrs. Mary Jones. Shortly after he was released from prison, he drafted a letter that could be sent to all his workaday supporters: a form letter, a template. I didn't learn this until recently when, reading Elmer Gertz's account of the case, I came across the text of the letter, addressed *Dear Friend*; not a word-for-word rendering of the one he sent her but a recognizable facsimile.

It took me a moment to absorb this. My mother wasn't special. The letter wasn't unique. And as I put down Gertz's book and leaned back in my chair, I felt hurt on my mother's behalf. It was as if Nathan Leopold had slighted her, and slighting her, he'd slighted me. He'd taken back something he'd given, recognition conferred then denied, and now she was cast off—worse, forgotten—replaced by an anonymous *friend. Finally the day has come.* Leopold's letter had nothing to do with my mother, Mrs. Nathan Shinner, Harriet Shinner, née Alter. There was no code to crack, no secret message. She wasn't hidden between the lines. I'd inflated her, and by extension myself, and now he brought us down together.

TWELVE

Nathan Leopold died of a heart attack in 1971, thirteen years after the Illinois Parole Board granted his release. He was sixty-six. "Nathan F. Leopold of 1924 Murder Case Is Dead," the *New York Times* headline read. The obituary rehashed the details, and noted his post-prison accomplishments: he earned a master's degree at the University of Puerto Rico, taught mathematics, and raised money for the Church of the Brethren. He was survived by his widow, whom he'd married in 1961 (was she a beard? Did he, in his dying days, dream of Loeb?), and two brothers, who, to avoid publicity, had changed their names. He donated his eyes to the University of Puerto Rico eye bank. My mother died in 1981. She was fifty-six. Her death went unremarked, except for the usual qualifiers: *Loving daughter. Beloved wife. Devoted mother.* A year later my father, on his own, placed a one-line memorial in the newspaper: *Ma, We miss you*, and although I did, I felt ambushed when I came across it. He hadn't even asked. The clippings are stashed in a U-Haul box in the closet of my study, along with photos, report cards, ticket stubs, bank statements, receipts, a running tally of the everyday. When I get the urge to snoop around in my past, I dump it all out and sift through the disintegrating contents, ambushed once again.

Tax Time

SIGHTING

I go to my accountant, this accountant, because he reminds me of my father. He brings him up. I thought of your father last week, he said. He said this to me when Ann and I went to see him for our taxes. He was punching numbers into the computer. We were sitting across from him at his big, messy, mahogany-colored desk. I'm uncomfortable at this desk, spread out like a landmass between us, because I feel like I haven't yet legitimately—with my own income—entered the ranks of the middle class. My shabby W-2s prove it. But I can't claim to be anything other than middle class either. I'm a middle-class woman who inherited her working-class-turned-middle-class father's money, earned first from owning a laundromat, and later selling furniture seven days a week out of chintzy model homes. Really? I say, soft-pedaling my interest because I don't want to appear overeager or worse, needy. It feels like a sighting. Steve's (not his real name) seen my father roaming around at the edges of his memory, and he files a report. I wait for him to offer up his choice morsel. It's not that he teases me, but he doesn't deliver right away either. He has a comic's sense of perfect timing.

Or maybe it's just that at the same time he mentions my father, he's also perusing my interest and dividend statements—one of which is from Calvert, a socially responsible investment firm that, to my consternation, hasn't done so well lately, meaning I've squandered my father's money for the dubious idea of responsible investing and my accountant is about to nail me for it—and his recollection will unfold in good time.

To meet with him, I drive to Northfield, a suburb thirty-five minutes from my house in good traffic, every year in early spring. Steve does my taxes, makes me penalty proof, talks about my father. If I pay too much for him to do my taxes, as a friend once implied, a friend who said that if I went to her accountant I would only pay half what I pay now, this is what I'm paying for. I'm paying to keep my father alive. The price this year is $365, up ten dollars from last. Some people go to synagogue and recite the Kaddish in memory of their loved one. I go to my accountant. He's one of the few people left who remember him, who have memories of my father distinct from mine. Every year he resurrects a memory, and even if he resurrects the same memory, or a version of the same memory year after year, I appreciate it. His memories become my own.

Or that's what I tell myself. I'm proprietary. I reassemble all the far-flung pieces of my father, including the ones he gave to someone else, because somewhere, in the deepest part of me, I feel they are rightfully mine, even if, in another part of me, I know that that's impossible.

I was telling somebody about our poker game, Steve says, handing me back the statements. Steve, who used to be my father's accountant, used to play poker with a bunch of *alter kockers*, rough-edged, self-made Jews, one of whom was also my father; they were all, at the very least, thirty years Steve's senior. Steve is rough-edged too, even though he wears expensive though casual, perfectly hung pants and matching, muted shirts, possibly Italian. He has slim hips, a flat stomach, a belt of polished leather. His backside is small and rounded. He probably works out, at five-thirty in the morning, with other overworked, type-A overachievers. Referring to some arcane and, to his mind, stupid regulation in the tax code, he calls George Bush a fucking moron.

POKER

Was he a good player? I ask. Despite my effort at nonchalance, at the mere mention of my father I'd felt a surge of tears—quickly squelched—and on his behalf fished for a compliment instead. My father was a good player; I already knew that. When I was a kid, we used to play gin. He'd keep track of the cards I picked up from the discard pile, and on his turn he'd never toss out anything of the same suit. He was not a father who let his daughter win. Steve answers by telling me what a good player *he* was—not that I'm bragging, he says, don't take this the wrong way, and then adds that my father was sharp as well. Your father knew how to play, he says knowingly, noddingly. They were the good players, and the others were pathetic. But he kept quiet, he says, because who was he, the young one, the upstart, to say anything to these guys. Your father was disgusted with them, he says, suggesting that at one time or another my father probably gave someone—Maury Zitlin, Irv Witt, Fox Williger, Lou Singer—a mouthful. I have no trouble imagining it: quick to blow up, my father ended up in many angry, defensive confrontations. Still, I take posthumous pride in his skill and reputation, as if the shine from his card-playing acumen has rubbed off on me and I'm basking in the light of a revered tradition.

AUNTS

Relax, Steve says. I'm nervous about my taxes. Now that I organize my aunt's taxes, my great-aunt's, who this tax season turned ninety-eight, I can't seem to keep track of my own. Steve has an aunt also. Ten years younger than my aunt, this aunt has eleven nieces and nephews to look after her affairs and pay her expenses. She doesn't have a cent. Every year we talk about our aunts, about their bilious temperaments, about the expense of caretakers, about how they, the aunts, live on and on, enlivened by their meanness. Both our aunts are sharp as tacks, which they don't hesitate to stick into you. They've moved his aunt out of her apartment, he says; now she lives in a palace, the word practically exploding from his lips. She's patently ungrateful, he implies.

My aunt lived like royalty too. At least according to my father. He used to call her The Queen. Widowed, wealthy, martyred, entitled, she sat on her throne in her thirty-fourth-floor apartment above Lake Shore Drive, watching her investments accrue interest. My father worked as a cashier at a car wash. *Your father called me The Queen*, she told me, as if it were the nicest thing ever said to her. Twenty years later, however, her investments have taken a dive, and she's lost her title.

When his aunt complains, Steve says, he threatens her with the death stick. He holds it over her head. I see it materialize, a wand of great potency, making its final and glorious descent. Ann and I laugh. Where can we get one? Somewhere in the conversation I let out that my aunt's name is Etta, and he, in a triumph of coincidence and one-upmanship, says that his is Yetta, Yetta Etis. Etta Fefferman, née Zaslowsky. Yetta Etis, née Garfinkel. Can you tell they're Jews? he says. *Our* names are appropriately assimilated, mine perhaps overly so. I know of one other Jew named Peggy, and imagine a small society of others, fifties-born Jewish girls—their parents aggressively American—named Margaret, Patty, Maggie, Peggy, for girls who came over on another boat. As for Shinner, my father's name was originally Shinitzky; but a month before his marriage, at the urging, I suspect, of my mother, who did not want to be saddled with such a foreign-sounding name, suggestive of shtetls and head coverings, he changed it. Steve's last name is Silver.

He's still talking about his aunt. Have you ever noticed, he says, how they—he means old people—take out their keys long before they get home and jangle them in their hand? He says the word *jangle* with particular distaste. Yes, yes, Ann and I say, in a rush of recognition. Etta does that—or used to, when she went out—too. Across from me in the passenger seat, blocks (if not miles) from her apartment, she'd fish in her purse for her keys while I looked on with mute and growing annoyance. The elderly, it seems, prepare for their arrival long before they get there. It's as if the trip were over as soon as you begin the return, and that's the part we can't stand. The foreshortening. I hate that jangling, Steve says, and in that moment we hear it: the far-off clanging of a distant gatekeeper. If I ever jangle my keys, he says, shoot me.

Finally, we go back to the taxes, and Steve reassures me that I'm prepared for our appointment, I have everything he needs, and if not, if I've made some terrible mistake or omission, we'll fix it. He has pale skin, blue eyes, washed-out red hair. His trim beard is red and gray. He seems, simultaneously, younger and older than I am. In his swiveling leather chair, he could be a father, a brother, a friend. He grew up, or so I remember, in the same neighborhood as I did, went to the same grammar school, Hannah Greenbaum Solomon, was possibly even a member of the same congregation, A. G. Beth Israel; but while my house, a one-story ranch, seemed simple and straightforward, as if, by its very layout, it could harbor no intrigue, his, a two-story, red-brick Georgian, formidable and silent, at least as I picture it, was full of secrets. We'll fix it, Steve says, with a smile suggesting that nothing, in that instant, is insurmountable, and I feel my anxiety melt away.

SIGNS

Steve reminds me of my father in a physical way too. Every year he gets older. He's getting older in the way that certain Jewish men get older. I can see it, sitting across from him, the way you can see it only when you see somebody once a year. Over the weekend a colleague of Ann's died. He'd just had surgery on his Achilles tendon, and was in the shower when he called out to his cousins. Within three minutes he was dead. Did he see it coming? Did a storm gather overhead? I can see it coming on Steve. I can see the years accruing, the fatigue setting in, the sorrows and disappointments, a certain Semitic sag of the face and chin, leavened by a sharp wit, good wine, an occasional par on the golf course, accomplished children, an Italian wife, and the fact that with Ozzie Guillen as manager of the White Sox, things are looking up.

I didn't see it coming on my father. I refused to see it. It took me by surprise. I saw him once a week, and the week before he had his stroke we had breakfast together at the Barnum and Bagel restaurant, where, over lox and onions, he told me that the day before, his hand had gone numb and he'd dropped a cup of coffee—a sure sign, I knew, I knew even then, if I'd wanted to see it.

FINGERS

I notice Steve's fingers. They're wound around the pencil as he scribbles some figures from the computer. They're short and stubby, like my father's, and impeccably groomed. Does he get his nails done? Is that a vanity he permits himself? My father had a manicure once when he was seeing Rose, and at the time I saw it as jumping ship. He was, by slapping on some nail polish, trying to abandon his class for Rose's, Rose, a woman who subscribed to the symphony, and tried to break his use of double negatives. He was also dandying himself up, something I wondered if he'd ever done for my mother when she was alive. When he told me, with an impish shrug of his shoulders, that he'd fallen asleep at the symphony, I was pleased.

Steve puts down the pencil. He punches in a few more numbers and furrows his face as he attacks the keys. My father never sat at a computer. He counted on his fingers, he computed in the air. His fingers would paw the imaginary numbers in front of him until they reached a conclusion. Sometimes, when food got stuck in his mouth, he'd run his thumb and forefinger over his dental plate to dislodge it. He seemed to make a show of it, like his thumb was a fine-tuned instrument. He took a certain pride in being crude. My fingers, like theirs, are short and stubby too.

GAINS AND LOSSES

Perhaps Steve, certified public accountant, is like a father. The tax man, before whom every year you spread out your papers, your receipts, your tattered scribblings and calculations. You show him your gains and losses, your business expenditures, your list of charitable contributions and deductions, and with equal parts wizardry and math, he tells you what it all amounts to, how it all adds up. Look, you say, or want to say, how much I gave away last year, to the Crossroads Fund, Lambda Legal Defense, the Lesbian Community Cancer Project, the Chicago Women's Health Center, Amnesty International, Grinnell College (your alma mater), WBEZ, (your local public radio station), the National Coalition for the Homeless, Housing Opportunities and Maintenance for the Elderly, an organization for which, ever since your father died and they came and took his furniture (which the Salvation Army rejected), you've always had a soft spot. Not to mention (but you do, you have to, for the deduction) the in-kind donations—household goods, books, clothes, recycled birthday presents—you made to the Brown Elephant resale store. You want to impress him with your generosity, which you well know isn't generous enough. Is it generous if you're not giving anything up? You seek his approval, not as a client but as a child. Have I donated enough money? Have I done good works? Will I be inscribed in the Book of Life? Did you sell any stories this year? he asks, and though you did, how can you tell him you got paid with two free copies of a journal he's never heard of? You sink, crestfallen, in your chair; You're a failure, you think he thinks, but he turns his blue eyes back to the computer and does his best to hide his condemnation.

My father, my real father, not Steve, the ersatz father, the once-a-year stand-in, thought I could do no wrong, as my aunt, The Queen, once said. In his eyes—by turns warm, mischievous, weary, wounded—my approval rating was 100 percent. He approved of everything he knew about me, but he didn't know everything. He didn't know, for instance, that Ann is my primary beneficiary, that down the road she'll inherit what's left of the money he left me, that she'll get everything I've got. That everything I've got, all these years later, is less than I had.

GATHERING

Steve's father died a long time before mine did. Maybe he's looking for a father too. Maybe that's why he played cards with a bunch of *alter kockers* thirty years his senior, most of whom didn't know a thing about poker. None of them, singly, reminded him of his father, but together they formed a quorum. Maybe that's why he talks about my father. Together we can conjure up a father between us. We can whistle one up. An old Jewish guy, grizzled, gruff, argumentative, proud, vulnerable, savvy, who once a year makes his congenial appearance around the tax table, who, with little prodding, deals a hand or two from the deck. The fathers gather together, mine, Steve's, Steve himself, who decorates his office walls with the emblems of fatherhood—photos of his children smiling out at him, two sons and a daughter; finger paintings, temperas, a mixed-media construction of a dinosaur in Jurassic Park; a certificate honoring him as Little League coach of the year; framed ticket stubs to a White Sox playoff game that, I imagine, he and his kids went to together—and surrounded by these ghosts and trinkets, we turn to the year's evidence and do the taxes.

REFUND

Do I see it coming? Do I see the end? Not in the foreseeable future, but how far can I see ahead? I see tax season after tax season, year after year of visits with Steve. Ann has had breast cancer; once we had a car accident and landed in a ditch. My aunt lives on, but she tells me she won't see her next birthday. She's been saying this for years, perhaps to thwart the gods above, and I used to reassure her, but now I know better than that. My father had a stroke on the Dan Ryan Expressway, and four weeks later he was dead. Steve is still running the numbers. Ann and I sit murmuring to each other on our side of the desk. I suck on a toffee from the candy dish. Where should we go for lunch? she says. Finally Steve looks up from the computer and smiles at me again. Good news, he says.

You're getting a refund. Great, I say, relieved and greedy. Now that I don't have to pay, I wonder if I'll get a windfall.

About two hundred dollars, he says.

Two hundred dollars?

A minute ago I was worried about paying, and now I'm disappointed, as though it's not much more than loose change.

Steve rises from his desk. We gather our papers together. Maybe the White Sox are for real, I say, but Steve shakes his head as if to say he's beyond caring. I'll mail you the forms, he says, accompanying us out of the office. He pats his hands on his pants. Call if you have any questions, but of course he means about our returns. I'm waiting, but he makes no mention of my father, and in this moment I know, as I know every year, that this is about taxes, and that Steve is my accountant, and that if we have, ever so briefly, conjured up a father, that father has been sucked back into the bottle and the bottle has been capped, and now the daughter, with her shopping bag full of the year's accounting, the promise of a modest refund, and a toffee wrapper crumpled in her pocket, has been sent back home. We shake Steve's hand. Then Ann and I head to the hallway, and for a second I feel that drop in my stomach as the elevator pulls us down.

Mood Medicine

She takes mood medicine. That's what her caretaker calls it. *She* didn't call it anything at first. I'm not depressed, she said. I'm not crazy. Once a day she gets 30 milligrams. The caretaker doles it out with a glass of water, and she looks at the pills as if interrogating them, as if they're nothing short of trash, before throwing them in her mouth and downing the water in one long, torturous gulp. Then she swipes the back of her hand across her lips: finished. She's nearing a hundred, and before the mood medicine she looked up to the ceiling, the sky, the heavens, and asked God to take her. God, who she also called The Man Upstairs. Please, God, she cried, why must I suffer? I can't take it anymore. I've lived long enough. She sneaked a look at you as she said this, just to make sure those at ground level were listening too.

Now she says—*now,* since the mood medicine—I'm getting along, followed by a coquettish laugh. She's become a flirt. A Buddha. She sits in her chair wearing a pastel housecoat, with a sea-green blanket on her lap. She looks beached, becalmed. She tells you she has a taste for a club sandwich. Like a pregnant woman, she adds, amused with herself. Her feet, slid into faux-sheepskin slippers by the caretaker, are perched on a footstool. Knee-highs hover around her mottled ankles. She has bad circulation. She has all her marbles. That's my problem, she said, before the mood medicine.

Her doctor prescribed it. Don't you get depressed? she asked him: an accusation, a dare, a laying down of the gauntlet. Her blue eyes were like ice picks. She could have killed him. He did get depressed. He had reasons. He was from the former Yugoslavia. His father had dropped dead of a heart attack there. Oh . . . she softened. Her heart went out to him. She forgave him. Doctor, she said. It was a term of endearment. She couldn't pronounce his last name. Lasarevic. It was too foreign. He was wearing black—he would wear it for a year—which, as she eyed him up and down, made him look very handsome.

* * *

She had reasons too. She'd married a merchant, originally from Montana, who sold rawhides. When they met, she was seventeen and working as a typist for Dun & Bradstreet. She rode the streetcar downtown. At night she liked to dance. She attracted men. This one was rich. She was beautiful. The parents happy. At the wedding she wore a tiara. Then she had a baby, a girl. She was eighteen. It took three days. The baby was retarded. The husband branched into bedding. He sold sheets and towels to hospitals. He imported Hudson Bay blankets. She made bread and lamb and blintzes. Her father, a peddler, fell off his cart and died. They moved from Chicago to Berwyn, a suburb. The daughter stopped talking. The husband philandered. Their bank account burgeoned. They drove west in a Cadillac with a black chauffeur. They bought silver from the Indians. They went to Banff. They moved to Skokie, another suburb. She made Bundt cake. They bought a house in Miami. The mangoes were delicious. He went deep-sea fishing. He mounted the fish on the wall in Skokie. She descended the stairs to do laundry. She wore shirtwaist dresses. He planted Big Boy tomatoes. The floors were spotless. They had four French poodles. The daughter's hair fell out. The husband carried on with the secretary. She stuffed capons. They bought a tree in Israel. The husband died of colon cancer. The daughter died of esophageal cancer. She moved in with a niece. The niece died of thyroid cancer. She sold the house in Skokie. She sold the Hudson Bay blankets. She kept the beveled perfume bottles. She moved back to the city. She bought blond wood furniture. She made a yearly donation to Little City. She read the *National Enquirer*. She watched the Jerry Lewis muscular dystrophy telethon. She baked a potato for dinner. Her blood pressure went up. Her younger brother died. Her older sister died. She was fitted for a dental bridge. She bought a baby-blue cashmere sweater to match her eyes. Her eyesight failed. Her friend Lake broke her back in the bathroom. Her friend Margaret had a stroke. Her friend Mae lost her memory. She got shorter. She couldn't read. She renewed her lease. She broke her rib. She ate half a banana. Is there any mail? she asked. Why didn't you call me? Stay five more minutes. She couldn't sign her name.

* * *

Her mood medicine is Celexa. It celebrates happiness, x-es out anxiety. Its logo is a genie, a jack-in-the-box, sprung, come free, arms outstretched to the world in joy and release. Both genie and pill are seashell pink, and like a seashell pressed to your ear, there's the whisper of a promise, *you'll be okay, you'll be okay*. It's the color, too, of certain bridesmaids' dresses and, incidentally, the upholstery of her blond wood dining room furniture.

There is, of course, a method to both name and color. The letter *C*, say branding experts, suggests efficiency and effectiveness, while *X*, with its high-tech connotations, is fast-sounding, implying, whether true or not, fast-acting. As for color, a design critic in a 1998 *Washington Post* article put it this way: "White is for cheap generics; pastels are increasingly used for stress relievers; bright colors try harder—they are for the . . . powerful, the expensive, the new."

On its website, Celexa shows beatific people of various ethnicities next to dandelion puffs, ocean swells, butterflies, falling maple leaves. Some are hugging a loved one. One has her arms stretched wide like the genie itself. Many have their eyes either raised skyward or looking straight at you with frank, happy expressions. The skies are mostly, but not totally, blue, perhaps to suggest that Celexa, while highly effective, can't do everything. There may always be a—harmless—cloud or two on the horizon. No matter: these people can handle it. On Celexa, life is declawed. There are no hurricanes; no lashing rains or storm surges. In one frame there's an outsize seashell, invitingly pink on the inside and bigger than the sky, the beach, the sea itself.

* * *

Sunny pink Celexa. It helps her mood, but she's not happy to take it. She calls it the one-and-a-half. That's because she takes one and a half pills a day. At first she took one pill a day, 20 milligrams, but it had no effect. The doctor upped the dosage to 30. Calling it the one-and-a-half is the closest she comes to acknowledging it; the closest she comes to admitting she's taking an antidepressant at all.

She's against depression. It's not in her vocabulary. It's not in her vocabulary, that is, as a disease, an illness; just as a condition of life. I'm so depressed, she says, pronouncing it dee-pressed, as if to emphasize its depths. She expects to be depressed. She's made periodic visits to the doctor—her GP—to treat it. She tells him her troubles. She says she's blue. She says that the members of her family—the two surviving—have their own lives now. That's the way it is, she says, meaning she wishes it weren't. By this time the doctor is holding her hand. Doctor as healer, rabbi, counselor, confidant. Those are the roles she assigns him. She likes older, avuncular types, which, as she's gotten older, as one by one they've either died or retired or been paralyzed by a stroke, has become impossible. Drs. Lasarevic, Berkson, Hyman, and, almost unbelievably, Dr. Doctor, the first one in the lineage and the one, burnished by time, she speaks of the most reverently. The Ur-doctor, with whom the others, unknowingly, compete.

It's the current one and the youngest by far in the line of successors, though he too holds her hand and even, she reports, gives her an occasional kiss on the cheek, who dared to prescribe the antidepressant. Who, when the Celexa wasn't working, upped it to one-and-a-half times the original dosage.

She's depressed as hell, he told you.

You call it the one-and-a-half too. You conspire with her to hide her depression from herself. It's a mouthful, so much harder to say than the smooth-sounding Celexa, so much harder and easier too. You feel foolish and ashamed as you say it. Have you taken the one-and-a-half today?

Sometimes she threatens not to take it. That's usually when she's sick (bronchitis, arthritis, bladder infection) and, therefore, depressed. She's afraid of death; she's afraid, even as she's preparing to welcome it. Call that doctor, she says, struggling to remember the name, and when you offer Kevorkian, guessing at her familiarity with talk-show culture, she nods yes, not realizing, or perhaps not caring, that Dr. Death is in jail now. When the caretaker comes with the mood medicine, she shakes her head in disgust. Don't be ridiculous, she seems to be saying. What do I need that for when I'm on my way out. The caretaker slips you a look, suggesting they go through this often. I don't want it, she repeats, this time to you, presumably so you can register the direness of her circumstances, and *then* you can urge her to take it. She does.

* * *

Antidepression doesn't come cheap. A month's worth of Celexa costs $106.56. Insurance provides a five-hundred-dollar annual drug allowance, and then she's on her own. I need the Bank of England, she says, knowing it's not coming to her aid anytime soon. Celexa, Norvasc, Prilosec, Claritin, the expense of caretaking not covered by insurance, and the bill adds up. Do I have to take money out? she mouths, not wanting the caretaker, who's making dinner, to overhear. Yes, you nod, and when she asks how much, you answer in a voice loud enough for her—and therefore the caretaker—to hear you.

She used to be rich. There used to be a building downtown with her husband's name on it, which is her name too, although she doesn't refer to it like that. His name, his monument. The Fefferman Building, she says with a bemused laugh, like she can't believe that it actually had something to do with her life—or maybe it's that she can't believe it used to have something to do with her life and now it doesn't. You find it hard to believe as well. You try to imagine that Montana moniker carved in stone on a South Loop warehouse storing sheets, towels, pillowcases, shams, dust ruffles, blankets, and other textiles, and square this with the shrunken antiquity sitting before you. She's survived, but the building is gone.

* * *

How depressed is she? You take the depression self-screening test. You take the test for her. It's on the Celexa website. You've been there many times. You've been there so many times, in fact, you think they'll think you're depressed. It's her, you want to tell them, in case someone out there is logging in your email address and monitoring your hits. As if depression were, after all, a source of shame, or, at the very least, a failing you must distance yourself from. You feel like one of those people who phone a crisis hotline—for instance, the teen line where you once worked as a telephone counselor—and say they're calling for a friend.

You are the great-niece. She is the great-aunt. She is your grandmother's sister. Your grandmother is dead. Your mother too. All the others as well. Two generations picked clean. Two generations and forty-five years apart, you and she are left together in Chicago (the other surviving relative, your brother, is in California). She lives in her own apartment, with twenty-four-hour care. You are, as it were, the off-site manager. The caretakers cook, clean, shop, do the laundry, make the bed, measure out the blood pressure, acid reflux, and mood medicines; comfort her when she awakens frightened from a dream; water, divide, and repot the plants; bathe her; moisturize her skin; hem her housecoats; kiss her forehead at the end of their shifts. On occasion they sing her a song. You wonder, in a dark corner of your mind, if they wipe her rectum. For your part, you call every day; manage her finances; buy her lavender soap, croissants, cream soups; come once a week and pay her bills. When you kiss her good-bye, often as not she starts to cry.

The self-screening test is simple. It covers the biggies: sleep habits, appetite, decision-making, self-image, thoughts of death or suicide. Never mind your own confused feelings about her depression. About whether anyone in her circumstances—anyone who is widowed, homebound; who has outlived a child, has impaired sight and hearing, chronic pain, dwindling resources—could not help being depressed. Persistent depression "is not a normal part of aging," according to the National Institute of Mental Health. But if the salient risk factors for late-life depression, according to the Celexa website, are social isolation or lack of support, female gender, bereavement, chronic illness, disability or disabling illness, and financial strain, why isn't it normal? When you rant about this to a friend, she gently reminds you, Pain is normal, but that doesn't mean you shouldn't alleviate it.

Of course, you say, feeling chagrined, as if you had actually considered depriving her of the antidepressant—which you hadn't.

Never mind, as well, your own—minor—depressions. Never mind that the first time you tried to go to a therapist—so long ago now that you can't remember what for—she declined to take you as a client because, she discreetly said (and with no further explanation), it wasn't a good match. Never mind how that made you feel—that your problems were uninteresting, unimportant; that you were a depressed bore. Or that the second time you went, many years later, you stopped after one visit because you realized you didn't need a therapist to tell you that you were sad and depressed over your father's recent death.

Never mind all this. You try to answer as she would. As she would, pre-Celexa. You try to be her.

I awaken more than once a night and stay awake for twenty minutes or more. I feel sad more than half the time. I eat much less than usual and only with personal effort. I have virtually no interest in formerly pursued activities. I believe I cause problems for others. I think of suicide or death several times a week for several minutes.

You feel sneaky. Excited. You wish you could say more empathetic, but you can't. You resist the impulse to look over your shoulder. You imagine a sudden flashing on the screen as your (her) scores are tallied, and instead of a prize at the end, a DVD player, say, a message pops up: BINGO! You've Got Depression!

And so she does. When the numbers are added up—the Celexa website, ever helpful, does this for you—her score is 17: moderate to severe depression.

You're vindicated and oddly disappointed. Her depression is confirmed, but not enough. Only scores over 18 qualify as (unequivocally) severe depression, nothing moderate about it. You find that you want to cast her in the role of martyr—a role, in fact, she's worn quite comfortably on her own for decades—even if, in this case, it's the martyrdom of debilitating mental illness. Perhaps you want to cast yourself in the role of martyr too. Her depression, before it was treated with Celexa, was overwhelming—to you. You were exhausted by your inability to do anything about it. By her sometimes truculent refusal to face it. Depressed as hell, her doctor'd said. You remember your relief when he said it.

But your self-pity is not only about her depression. I'm a burden to you, she's said on more than one occasion, and you've felt burdened having to deny it. She *is* a burden. She's an enormous responsibility, even though you've parsed it out to underpaid employees. Like her, you've wondered why she's lived so long. You wonder how much longer she'll go on. You wonder what will happen if her money runs out. The actuarial tables, according to your financial counselor, say that if a person lives to ninety-five, life expectancy increases by five more years. How did you end up in this position? You and she were never close. Once, when your father needed a job, her husband, the dry-goods merchant, refused to help him. She had a boxer, a dog named Melody, who reared up and frightened you as a child. You've been afraid of boxers ever since. You feel ashamed by these thoughts. You'll never know how much I love you, she says, her voice full of pleading and fervor. You tell yourself it's as much a privilege to help usher someone out of this life as it is to bring someone in. You believe this. It doesn't matter. Your high-mindedness is no match for your anger. When you don't feel ashamed by your thoughts, you feel entitled to have them.

* * *

Now, a year after she started Celexa, she has breakthrough depression. Little leakages in her line of defense. Celexa's a wall, a barrier, but it can't hold everything back. It can't stop the days from accruing, and the diminishments from piling on.

I'm useless, she says while you're writing the checks. Her head nearly drops to the table.

I'm paying the Visa bill, you say in an attempt to rouse her, to suggest she's the one in control and you're merely carrying out orders.

Good, she says, but she couldn't care less.

Nobody needs me, she says, both to express the acuteness of her feelings and to elicit your rebuttal. It has come to you that *you* need her, as someone—the only one, actually—from a previous generation who loves you, but you do not say, have never said, anything about this. You're hampered, not only by the awkwardness of your affection but by some resentment that makes you want to withhold it, and your denial is more rote than reassuring.

She turns to ask God why she's still around, and because, presumably, she gets no answer (He's no more helpful than you are), takes the pills—upped now to two a day, 40 milligrams—the caretaker hands her.

Are these for my mood? she asks, slightly bewildered.

* * *

She doesn't go out anymore. She's afraid of the elements. She's afraid of falling. She's afraid of getting tired. She's afraid of being cold. She goes to the doctor for her annual checkup once every two months. He wants to see me, she says. He listens to her heart. He prescribes a diuretic. He kisses her cheek. He tells her she's his oldest patient. She asks about his baby daughter. She asks, with her flirtatious laugh, if he's going to have another. She asks for free samples. At home she takes long naps curled up like a single-celled organism. After she wakes up, she says that she hasn't slept. She waits for the phone to ring. Her former cleaning lady calls twice a day. I was very good to her, she tells you, suggesting the twice-a-day phone calls are her due. Occasionally she makes a call herself. She calls the fishmonger at Treasure Island. What's good today? Do you have that fish, the one I like, tilapia? Is it fresh, I only buy the best, she says, halfway between a statement and a threat.

When you have a cold, she calls you.

What are you taking for it? she says. Don't go out, she warns.

She reminds you to pay her quarterly taxes. She asks if she has enough money. What's my balance? she whispers. She sinks her chin into her chest. She works the fingers of one hand with the other. She looks out the window. Are they playing today? she asks, glancing toward Wrigley Field. Her blue eyes slide inward. She shakes her head, as if she were trying to understand something, as if the pieces would fall into place. A shadow crosses over her. There's a swoop of wings coming close, then veering past. She shrinks away from it. So many birds, she says with a start, afraid, as one flies by, that it will hit the glass.

Intimate Possession

My lover and I talk, on occasion, about where we want to be buried. The occasion, usually, is someone else's death. We talk about this, not while we are among the mourners waiting to shovel a scoopful of dirt into S.'s son's open grave, standing in line with his eighth-grade classmates, girls wearing high-heeled sandals in the thirty-degree February cold, boys in below-the-waist saggy pants. We talk about it leaving the cemetery, the heat turned up in our Toyota. Would you want to be here? I ask. But I'm caught up in the sentiment of the moment, and I don't really want to be here. Here is Rosehill, and it's too ecumenical.

A Jewish genealogy source notes that there are a significant number of Jews buried in the cemetery, and my friend A. told me that once an African-American door-to-door saleswoman for Rosehill, making a pitch for the place, said, "We have a large Jewish community." Still, its "we are the world" image just doesn't appeal. (Rosehill's parent company lays out its welcoming philosophy on its website: "From all branches of Judaism, Islam, Buddhism, Hinduism, Christianity and Native American religions to a variety of Asian, Hispanic and regional cultures, [we] are proud to serve diverse populations.") It turns out I'm sectarian in my burial leanings although not, I might add, in my choice of aboveground premises or partner. Ann, raised a Congregationalist, has long been a staunch nonreligionist. Pressed, she might say she's an atheist, but she's more spiritually inclined than I am. She takes her lessons from the natural world.

We also toss around future plans while taking a walk in Graceland, a historic cemetery in our neighborhood, where local luminaries are buried: Marshall Field, of department store fame; Potter Palmer, of the Palmer House Hotel; former Illinois governor John Peter Altgeld, best known for pardoning three of the Haymarket prisoners; railroad magnate George Pullman, who cut wages but not rents, and whose antilabor actions led to the 1894 Pullman strike; and renowned architects Louis Henri Sullivan (who designed the Getty mausoleum, also in Graceland, about which Frank Lloyd Wright said, "Outside the realm of music, what finer requiem?"), Daniel Burnham, and Mies van der Rohe. Once we went on a self-guided walking tour, stopping by the grave of William A. Hulbert, founder of the National Baseball League, marked by a stone baseball complete with stitched seams, which I expected to like because, after all, I like baseball. But the gray stone ball was too literal; I like my deaths made metaphorical, transcendent, dressed up with a line or two of poetry, hovered over by a mysterious statue. I want to shed a reflective tear or two, and you can't wring a tear, as they sort of say, from a stone. Give me Lorado Taft's bronze hooded figure *Eternal Silence*, standing over hotelier and early Chicago settler Dexter Graves: stark, evocative, watchful, inscrutable. But that was a commission, a famous artist, an important family, and Ann and I are ordinary, not the sort of people whose graves would be marked in this way.

But we do talk about being buried there. Ann does. She likes the trees—horse chestnuts, honey locusts, ginkgoes, flowering crabs—and the pond, called Lake Willowmere, with Canada geese. Goslings traipse after their parents, flickers stab at the trees for bugs. She likes the feeling of the place, where materials assume importance: monuments in white marble, bronze ornaments oxidized green, headstones hewn from granite, boulders that look as though they've been pushed out of the earth and deposited at precisely the right spot. It has personality, she says, everything's not the same.

I don't want to be buried in Graceland. Can I tell her? I do, and I see that crumple of disappointment. The place feels like Sauganash, the restricted neighborhood only ten minutes from the one I grew up in, where we used to go look at the decorations on Christmas Eve. First we would have porterhouse steak, a holiday treat because we—Jews, seasonal outcasts—had to celebrate somehow, and then we would get in the car and make the drive (across, wouldn't you know it, a set of tracks) to Sauganash, a neighborhood of outsize spruce trees festooned with Christmas lights where Jews and Blacks couldn't live but could come to admire. We crawled along in our Bonneville, pointing out the gaudy displays. Eventually a smattering of Jews came to Sauganash, though I don't know about Blacks, and that's what it seems like to me in Graceland. A white, well-moneyed, patrician place with a few Jews assimilated six feet under.

And then there's Westlawn. It's a Jewish cemetery, located just west of the city in Norridge. My parents are buried there. Maternal grandparents, a few aunts and uncles, a cousin who killed himself. (Traditionally, suicides have been denied burial in Jewish cemeteries, because the Talmud says life is a gift from God, and to willfully end it is a sin; but that stricture has loosened over time as rabbis came to see suicide as a mental health issue, or as one Jewish-sponsored website put it, "Suicides are . . . not in their right minds.") A small family, we don't take up too much real estate. A few days before my mother died, my brother and I drove out to purchase my parents' plots. They had always meant to, but never got around to it. So it was left to us. Dazed by loss and responsibility, I felt totally unequipped, but in the end took out the passbook and wrote a check. (If memory serves, the plots were about $700 each. Today the market price is $2,500.)

Westlawn's prosaic name, combining its two defining features, location and landscape, suggests its atmosphere too. It's a suburban cemetery, not just located in the suburbs but—with its mowed lawn, uniform headstones, sections called Evergreen, Daisy, Dahlia, Poppy evoking tidy subdivisions, graves decorated with pansies in the spring, dusty millers, coleus, and impatiens in the summer—a suburb in itself. Like Norridge, a largely middle-class, insular place where, over the years, even the pretensions have frayed. Westlawn hosts a few famous dead: Jack Ruby, Gene Siskel, Leonard Chess, and Abe Saperstein, onetime owner of the Harlem Globetrotters, whose wife, Sylvia, played mahjongg with my mother. If I were to be buried there, I would be consigned to a long decline in an uninspired netherland, the kind of place I've eschewed in the past and wish to avoid in the future. My parents are in the Eastlake section, which has a serpentine body of water traversed by a stone bridge. The bridge, now crumbling, is one of Westlawn's prized landmarks.

Do the residents of Norridge feel like we're intruding? Approximately forty-six thousand Jews are buried in Westlawn; Norridge has a living population of fourteen thousand. Of the latter, 32 percent are of Polish descent, 26 percent Italian, another 13 percent German. Sixty-nine percent of the residents are Catholic. There are two Baptist churches, two Lutheran, and one Catholic, and a Salvation Army outpost. Norridge's website makes no mention of Westlawn. On the "Links and Resources" page, under "Cemeteries," there are two options: "Catholic Cemeteries in Archdiocese of Chicago" and "Cemeteries of Illinois." The thirty-page City-Data.com report on Norridge (City-Data compiles comprehensive profiles of US cities, counties, and zip codes) doesn't refer to Westlawn either, but it does note two registered sex offenders among the citizenry. When I went out there recently and turned toward the cemetery, I saw a sign pointing to the Divine Savior Catholic Church and another to the Acacia Park Lutheran Church, but nothing showing the way to Westlawn.

Pariahs or paranoiacs? Is this invisibility willful, or am I all too willing to don the mantle of victimhood? Am I, as Israeli peace activist Uri Avnery has suggested about his fellow Jews, mired in a cult of suspicion? Jewish consciousness, Avnery says, is that of "a helpless, suffering people, waiting for the Cossacks to set upon us at any minute." I have not, during my association with Westlawn, been the target of anti-Semitism. No one has thrown an insult my way. But over the years I have not been able to shake a feeling of discomfort. Should I go as far as to say unwelcome? When I dealt with the Westlawn staff—by phone and over matters of grave decorations, costs, billing, i.e. money—they seemed aloof and chilly. There was, and still is, this stubborn internal refrain: *Those Jews, always haggling about money*. (Westlawn, to set the record straight, is owned by Temple Shalom in Chicago, and has been since 1956. I don't know anything about the demographics of its employees.) Demanding, querulous, haughty: I worried I'd become the sort of Jew defined by the age-old deprecations. It's not uncommon: the tormented take on the characteristics ascribed to them by the tormentors. A preemptive strike whereby you pillory yourself before someone else has a chance to. James Baldwin searingly describes this in his "Notes of a Native Son." He'd been working in a New Jersey munitions factory for a year during World War II. "It was the same story all over . . . in bars, bowling alleys, diners, places to live. I was always being forced to leave." On this particular night, he'd already been refused service at a diner. Next he went to a fashionable restaurant where he knew he wouldn't be served. When the white waitress approached him, eyes filled with astonishment, apology, and fear, his "fury flowed toward her"; he felt that "if she found a black man so frightening [he] would make her fright worthwhile." He wanted to grab her throat, but she wasn't close enough. So instead he picked up the only thing available, a mug of water on the table, and hurled it at her. He became her biggest fear, the rageful Negro.

Maybe you're wary now too. I've become a stereotype. Two stereotypes. The finagling Jew has teamed up with the paranoid one. (Toss in the neurotic as well: the JAP, the Jewish mother, Woody Allen.) But what happens when the Cossacks do set upon us? Sometimes a legacy gets fulfilled. On January 6, 2008, a Norridge resident defaced close to seventy of Westlawn's graves with anti-Semitic imagery and slogans. He drew a gallows with a Star of David hanging from it (borrowing from that uniquely American pastime, lynching). "Aryan Power," he wrote, "White Power," "Juden Raus" (meaning "Jews out!"—the phrase shouted by the Gestapo when rounding up Jews from their hiding places; also the name of a board game developed by the Dresden-based Günther and Company in 1936, in which players take turns rolling the dice and moving their pieces, naïf-like figurines in pointed medieval hats, like the ones Jewish men were forced to wear in the Middle Ages, to collection points from which they'll be shipped to Palestine. "If you manage to see off 6 Jews, you've won a clear victory!" the board proclaims. The Nazis disliked the "amusing little game," however, feeling it trivialized their grand agenda). The damage to Westlawn was upwards of $100,000. The staff, "shocked [and] nauseated," underscored the cemetery's "responsibility to those who lie here." My parents' graves were untouched.

* * *

For years I was the family keeper of the graves. My duties, as I defined them, were confined to armchair administration. I didn't pull weeds or visit on an annual basis. I paid the bills, chose the seasonal maintenance plans. Spring and summer plantings, cold-weather coverings. I tried to view this as a privilege—being the custodian of the dead—but as time went on I experienced it as a burden. Or maybe it's more apt to say I began to doubt the whole enterprise. Why was I prettying up my parents' and grandparents' graves? Why was I going back and forth over perpetual care or annual maintenance (in the long run, perpetual care is more cost effective, but in the short it costs a bundle), a blanket of juniper boughs for winter warming? The sly alliterative phrasing implied your relatives would be cold without it. Cold? You were meant to shudder. How could you allow that?

Was I improperly sensitized to the needs of the dead? Or perhaps our culture doesn't prepare us for such custodial duties? If I were a more observant Jew or Jew-cum-Buddhist (JewBu or JUBU, a term that came into use following the publication of poet Rodger Kamenetz's *The Jew in the Lotus*, which chronicles the fertile exchange between a diverse group of Jews and Buddhists, including the Dalai Lama, in the Tibetan enclave of Dharamsala, India, in 1990), would I have had some ready-made traditions to fall back on? (My martial arts training certainly opened a door in that direction.) The Japanese film *Departures* highlights the role of the *nokanshi*—loosely translated as "mortician" (an alternate translation is "encoffiner")—in the ritual preparation of the body for the coffin. Before the assembled family members and friends, who watch with acute attention, the *nokanshi* washes the body—"this washes away the weariness, pain, and cares of the world, and represents the first bath for one newborn in the next"—plugs the orifices, re-dresses the deceased in funeral garb, crosses the feet, stretches and folds the hands, applies makeup. "May I have your wife's favorite lipstick?" the *nokanshi* asks. The husband utters an anguished sound. The young daughter runs to get it. A meditative tenderness accompanies each gesture; all is done with exquisite delicacy and respect.

(Jews have a similar ritual, called *tahara*, the washing of the dead, performed by members of the *Chevra Kadisha*, or burial society, who, in preparing the body for burial, pour twenty-four quarts of water over it in a continuous flow.)

In the end I unwittingly fell back on the Bible. We didn't have a Bible in the house when I was growing up, and I've never read one. (Once Ann and I inadvertently stayed at a Christian fundamentalist lodge in the Boundary Waters region of Minnesota, and instead of candies, open Bibles were laid out on the nightstands on either side of the bed, as if the previous guests had stopped in the midst of reading and we were being invited to pick up where they had left off.) Many phrases in common parlance derived from the Bible: "ashes to ashes, dust to dust" is one of them. What the Bible actually says (Genesis 3:19) is "For dust thou art, and unto dust shalt thou return." The exact phrasing varies depending on which version of the Bible you read. This is from the Jewish Publication Society's 1917 translation of the Hebrew Bible. Ezekiel (28:18) speaks of ashes also: "I will bring thee to ashes upon the earth in the sight of all them that behold thee." The phrase "ashes to ashes, dust to dust" itself first appeared in the 1662 edition of the Book of Common Prayer as part of the liturgy for the Anglican burial service:

> Forasmuch as it hath pleased Almighty God of his great mercy to take unto himself the soul of our dear brother here departed, we therefore commit his body to the ground; earth to earth, ashes to ashes, dust to dust.

And, of course, there have been numerous literary and pop-culture references to ashes/dust over the centuries. Hamlet, in his increasing despair and disillusionment over the treacheries of his fellows, asks, "What is this quintessence of dust?" Jelly Roll Morton, in a New Orleans funeral march, sings, "Ashes to ashes / dust to dust / if the women don't get you / the liquor must," and Harold Pinter, over fifty years later, draws on the same lyrics in his 1996 play *Ashes to Ashes*, about, among other things, the terror of the Holocaust. And finally there's C. K. Williams's poem "Dust," an anthem to impermanence and materiality—shavings, chips, chalk, chaff, all manner of particulate—ending, in its last line, with "dust, darling dust."

Shinners, Shinitzkys, Feffermans, Alters: most were gone. *Committed to the ground.* I wouldn't object to a bed of impatiens every summer, but I wouldn't choose it. Better to leave that choice to someone more at ease with making it. I finally handed off my family's graves to my brother. He was suited to the task. The day before his wedding he had gone out to the cemetery to tell our parents about it. He'd wanted them to know the turn his life was taking.

* * *

I once met a woman who said that home is the place where your dead are buried. Where you'll lie too, I might add. B., ardent White Sox fan, lover of mob lore, lifelong Chicagoan, had her ashes scattered off Montrose Harbor in Lake Michigan. C., who left her much-loved New York for the first time at seventeen, the last time at forty-eight, and whose parents are buried there, avowed, when I repeated the remark to her, "I ain't coming back"; she wants to be tossed into the box canyon outside her front door in the high desert of northern New Mexico. B. W., a potter, the same, into her yard—from which you can see the Truchas Peaks—her remains eventually mixing with the carpet of ash outside her wood-fired kiln. Swedish physics professor Nils Strindberg died during an unsuccessful attempt to land a hydrogen balloon on the North Pole, and decades later his former fiancée, Anna Charlier, asked for the ashes of her heart to lie with him. And writer Francisco Goldman, in a 2011 *Paris Review* interview, noted that burying his wife, Aura, in Mexico made it sacred to him.

There are a scattering of Shinitzkys in Waldheim (founded in the late nineteenth century following a wave of eastern European immigration to Chicago), but that's not why I want to be buried there. It reminds me of the shtetl, a place I've never been, yet am quick to romanticize. A homey assortment of people, slurping soup together, reciting poetry; a place where Yentl wore pants, not because she'd had to disguise herself as a man, but because that was the custom and she wanted to. The shtetl, of course, is not one place but many; it's come to represent the aggregate of all eastern European Jewish towns, depleted first by pogroms and emigration and then wiped out during the Holocaust.

* * *

Shtetl: Yiddish for "small town," as distinguished from *shtetele*, tiny town; *shtot*, city; *dorf*, village; *yishev*, tiny rural settlement. Waldheim is an assemblage of such little towns, or as I think of them, neighborhoods, which together make an urban center, a thriving metropolis. Deposit me there, in one of the older sections, with arched gates representing Kletsk, Antopol, and Stolin in Belarus, Knyszyn in Poland, Brusilov and Pavoloch in the Ukraine. (These sections, often purchased by *landsmanschaften*, mutual aid societies set up to help Jewish immigrants with employment, health, funeral, and burial needs, assured that even in America you would be buried with your townsfolk.) When I go back to the earth, I can go back to my Ukrainian roots. The Ukraine, where three of my four grandparents reputedly came from, although there's no one left now to verify this and I've never done a genealogical search.

Waldheim has been subject to rehab, much like, in my mind, the shtetl itself. When I was growing up, my parents and many others of their class and generation would never have considered being buried there. In their eyes, the cemetery was unkempt and in disrepair. Low class. Their parents didn't come to America so that they, their children, could end up in a place like this. A 1975 article in the *Chicago Tribune* described graves covered with weeds, brush twelve feet high, and roads in dire need of resurfacing. Assimilation, lack of funds, the dismantling of the *landsmanschaften*—all were factors, Waldheim acknowledges, in the cemetery's decline.

But eventually Waldheim came around. Its website offers a reassuring picture of consolidated management, fiscal controls, ongoing maintenance, and renovation. The message is clear: don't worry, folks, there's money in the bank (a state-supervised endowment fund); we can mow the grass now, clear the rubble, straighten the markers, no more accidents like the one in 1986 when an unstable gravestone fell and crushed a four-year-old boy. Enter the gates, look around, the management beckons to the Jews of Greater Chicagoland, in a tone of hushed reverential noodging.

* * *

I don't own a plot in Waldheim, but I've inquired. I've inquired for Ann and me. Many years ago I made the fifteen-mile trip out there, part pilgrimage, part fact-finding mission. First I visited Emma Goldman's grave and the Haymarket anarchists' too, located in German Waldheim, also known as Forest Home, a separate cemetery from the Jewish one. Goldman, deported twenty years prior to her death, had requested burial next to her Haymarket heroes, and the US government, with nothing to fear once she'd died, let her back in. The day I went, her grave was adorned with mementos: a clover-shaped candle, a strand of red beads, rose petals, stones, purple statice, yellow mums, a button that read "ACORN: Association of Community Organizations for Reform Now." Goldman is flanked by other leftists in a section known as Dissenters' Row: Art Shields-Esther Shields, "Working Class Journalists"; Jack Kling-Sue Kling, "We Marched as One to Change the World"; Anna Sosnovsky Winokour, "Mother and Comrade"; Henry Winston, "They Took My Sight, but My Vision Remains." (Winston was sent to prison for Communist organizing, where he went blind from an untreated brain tumor.) Wandering past the gravestones, I felt a twist of admiration and sorrow. What would my marker say?

I drove on to Jewish Waldheim, minutes away. There I visited my grandparents' graves, my father's parents, Anna and Isadore Shinitzky. Anna, as I remember her, had a nervous, consuming energy; family rumors hinted that during World War II, after my father was drafted, she slit her wrists and needed shock treatments. Isadore, Izzy, Papa Busy was a tailor; good-natured, playful, but with a streak of sadness and anger; kinky hair and a receding hairline marked by two deep erosions on either side of his head, which have since shown up on my brother. I'm embarrassed to say that more than once I had to look up the spelling of their last name. I found it on Ancestry.com. Shinitzky. No *s* between the *z* and *k*: that's been the sticking point. (Immigrant names, in fact, often have variant spellings depending on factors such as family tradition, place of origin, language, shifting political boundaries, and who stamped your papers the day you passed through Ellis Island. My friend J. tells the story that her grandfather and his two brothers were all given the same name—Sam Leder, Sam Leder, Sam Leder—upon their entry into America.) My father's there too. He's gone back to being Nathan Shinitzky (as recorded in the 1930 census, one of Ancestry's sources), after all this time. After that long-ago decision to change his name and Americanize. Seeing his name, the name I never knew him by, took me by surprise. It reminded me yet again that our lives intersected for only a circumscribed period. That he lived almost half his life as a Shinitzky.

After stopping at the grave of Ann's cousin's partner, where P., in his bereavement, had planted morning glories around the stone—the same vine that grew rampant in our garden despite persistent efforts to eradicate it—I made my way to the cemetery office. A woman greeted me. I was surprised by her youth, as if only older people should work here, as if the office were a kind of way station before they settled in on a permanent basis. I pattered on about my connections to the cemetery in an effort to establish my credentials. I wanted to know about the policy regarding mixed couples, although I already had my suspicions. Judaism, at least certain branches, could be brittle and uncompromising. Years before at my mother's funeral, when I'd attempted to hug my Orthodox cousin, he'd shrunk from my embrace because Jewish law prohibited contact with someone who might be menstruating and therefore unclean.

The woman stiffened. I felt sleazy and vulnerable at the same time, like I was trying to trap her into admitting something I would later use against her. She was matter-of-fact, businesslike, not in the least regretful. Ann could not gain admittance here. We could not be buried together. (The same for P.; he could mourn here but not stay.) Waldheim was only for Jews, by birth or rabbinical conversion.

* * *

Non-Jews (Ann); half-Jews (in June 1996, a rabbi in the Israeli city of Sderot refused to bury a Russian immigrant child whose father was Jewish but whose mother was not); suicides; apostates (perhaps I would be considered one: I haven't renounced my Judaism, but I haven't practiced it either, and I'm mixed up with a *shikse*. "[Apostates] should not be buried near the graves of the righteous," notes *What Is Halacha?* an encyclopedia of Jewish law); *polacas* (a perjorative for eastern European Jewish women who, lured to South America at the turn of the nineteenth century with the promise of jobs, were forced into prostitution and denied burial in traditional Jewish cemeteries, and then founded their own): the Jews have a host of laws governing where the body may be put to rest.

The same with the book. Jews have long linked the two. Just look at the word *geniza*. As defined by *The Oxford Dictionary of the Jewish Religion*, a *geniza* is a "hiding place or storeroom . . . for the depositing of worn-out books and sacred objects . . . which must not be destroyed according to Jewish law. . . . Present-day Orthodox custom is to give burial to all such documents." It is thought to have roots in the Persian *ganj* (*kanj*), meaning "hoard or hidden treasure," and also in the Hebrew *niganz*, which, when written on gravestones, translates as "Here lies hidden this man." *Janazah*, its Arabic cognate, means "funeral." The term given such hoardings is *shemot*, or names; sacred papers bearing the name of God.

The body, the book. I had the opportunity to see the connections firsthand shortly after my visit to Waldheim, when I came across a sign above the photocopier at the Spertus Institute, a Jewish cultural center in Chicago. "Please DO NOT place any Shamos materials [a variant spelling of *shemot*] in the waste paper basket. Instead, place it on the tray labeled 'Shamos' on the table next to the copier. Thank you for your cooperation."

And what happened to the *shamos*, this discarded yet holy pile of photocopies? Once a year, the Spertus librarian told me, it was trucked to Waldheim Cemetery and buried. He showed me a clipping from the *Sentinel*, Chicago's onetime Jewish weekly, with a photo commemorating a recent burial. In the photo, taken at the cemetery, three men in suits, obviously in charge, stand smiling while behind them others sort through the boxes of *shamos*. This *geniza*, a joint effort of the Chicago Rabbinical Council and Piser Weinstein Menorah Chapels, "united the Jewish community," the caption says. Piser Weinstein is the funeral home that, years before, buried both my parents.

While the librarian was filling me in, while he was scurrying off and helpfully photocopying materials for me (not *shamos*, not discarded, kept all these years in a file folder labeled *Buried*), I felt a growing sense of anger. Do you mean, I said, if not to him then to the assembled minyan in my head, that a culture which buries cast-off papers in the cemetery would deny my lover a place there? Aimlessly, I glanced around as if searching for an explanation. Where is the decency—or to use the vernacular that arose from the Diaspora, when those selfsame people, cast out of Jerusalem, dispersed across the globe—where is the *menschlichkeit* in that?

* * *

All of this was many years ago. As if, bandying about the various cemeteries, I could get cosmic credit for confronting death while at the same time staving it off. Like my friend P., more than a decade older than I am, who, on the day she and her husband went to look at cemetery plots, ended up with a small patch in their local community garden instead. Things have changed. Ann was diagnosed with ductal carcinoma in situ (stage 0), or what we jokingly referred to as breast cancer lite. We bought a house in New Mexico. Crossing the Mississippi, we could get married in Des Moines if we wanted to. We're sixty now. Ann's made a decision. She's gone off without me, an independent agent. She's decided she wants to be cremated and, like our friends C. and B. W., have her ashes scattered in northern New Mexico. It's like the ocean, she says of the sweep of desert, and from our deck I look out at the undulating landscape to catch a glimpse of the ocean floor.

(She also has a file on her computer, which I haven't seen, noting the music she wants played at her funeral.)

How could she? I'm affronted on two accounts. We never discussed cremation. Never considered it. The Japanese cremate their dead. They hold the hyoid bone, located near the larynx, in special reverence, because it's said to resemble the Buddha in prayer; they place it in its own urn. The shores of the Ganges are aflame with the bodies of Hindus who, believing in the river's redemptive powers, come to die on its banks. In Great Britain, the cremation rate is over 70 percent. Our friend J., a retired nurse who volunteers at an end-of-life project in a small Colorado community, was a founder of its open-air cremation program. And several years ago, when Ann's parents died within three weeks of each other, we scattered their ashes over the Iowa ground her mother had once called the most beautiful place on earth.

Cremation is for other people, not for us. It's certainly not for Jews. In my parents' household, cremation was regarded with equal measures of dismissal and disgust. It filtered down to me as a dictum, another one of those things, like hunting and thrift store shopping, that Jews reputedly didn't do. The most obvious reason for this aversion is the Holocaust, but its roots go back long before that. Since biblical times, Jews have eschewed cremation—considered both *chukat hagoy* (a Gentile practice) and a desecration of the body—and chosen burial instead. Deuteronomy 21:23 says: "And if a man has committed a sin worthy of death and he is put to death and thou hang him on a tree, his body shall not remain on the tree but thou shalt surely bury him that day." Jewish law interprets this to mean that burial is sacrosanct (even the lowly criminal deserves it). It is both an honor and a mandate; a religious obligation. Maimonides codified this command in the twelfth century: "If the deceased gave instructions that his body not be buried, we ignore him, inasmuch as burial is a *mitzvah [duty]*, as the Torah says." My parents, of course, didn't know any of this (nor did I until recently). They were unschooled in Jewish law, probably had never heard of Maimonides, but they did hold some of the old beliefs that came to them, as Tevye sings in *Fiddler on the Roof*, under that conveniently vague and all-encompassing rubric of tradition.

(The extent to which Jews have traditionally viewed cremation as an anathema was clearly demonstrated in 2007, when the first crematorium in Israel, catering to the secular community, was destroyed by arson. ZAKA, a volunteer emergency response team "known for its sacred work in collecting human remains to ensure a proper Jewish burial," denied responsibility for the attack, but its founder went on to say of the crematorium, "It was an illegal activity, a desecration of the dead and I applaud the destruction of the building, which was destined to disappear in flames.")

* * *

Not only has Ann opted for cremation. She's opted out. She's left me on my own. From out of nowhere the words to a song I don't even know seem to find me. "Please don't let me be lonely." I'd imagined that we'd be lying next to each other in the cemetery, like we lie next to each other in bed, and if we wouldn't be chatting away as we sometimes do now, at least we'd have the tucked-in comfort of proximity. It's not for nothing that headstones in some eighteenth-century New England cemeteries were made to look like headboards, giving the illusion that death is but a little sleep from which you might awaken in the company of loved ones. Of course, what I'm really talking about is the succor this image provides me now; how it lessens the fear I feel anticipating our future separation. Settling on the cemetery, purchasing the plots, laughing giddily when the first swipe of the credit card is denied (the charge won't go through? fine!)—it could have been like planning a slumber party together.

But Ann wants her ashes scattered, and I want my place in the ground. *Here Lies This Jew.* Waldheim, I've decided, not without misgivings. What about my prior indignation? (There is another cemetery, Jewish, that takes all comers; it's closer than Waldheim, but somehow it feels like a foreign outpost.) I want a rabbi who welcomes everyone; a soupçon of Hebrew here and there, because the murmured sound of it, from my childhood, is familiar; a shovel passed from person to person as each one tosses dirt on my grave. The assembled will disperse. The sky will fill with and empty of clouds. The groundskeeper will slip the key in the lock. With thanks for the life just completed, I'll go solo into the dust.

Postmortem

After my father's funeral, his lady friend, R., said he'd had a good send-off. I knew what she meant. Piser Weinstein was packed, hardly an empty seat in the house. The rabbi, unknown to my father but briefed by my brother and me, was warm and well spoken. He was R.'s rabbi. My father was not observant. The rabbi had graciously met with us the day before the funeral at my father's apartment. I was impressed that he'd make a house call, to strangers no less, and on a Sunday. Tell me about your father, he said. I'd compiled a list of his traits on a yellow legal pad. In the den I read them off. Occasionally my brother and I disagreed. He was contentious, I said. Contentious? What do you mean, contentious? Argumentative. Okay, argumentative. The next day the rabbi stood before the assembled mourners. Nate was charming, the rabbi told us. He was funny. Hardworking. Frugal. A stickler. Yes, he could be argumentative. And the mourners, in agreement, laughed. He was, on occasion, hot-tempered. They nodded again. He was a simple man, not ostentatious. He loved his children. He loved the White Sox. He will be missed.

* * *

My father's brain is in a jar. That's how I imagine it. The curly mass squeezed in a Ball jar, sitting on a subterranean shelf somewhere in the basement of Evanston Hospital. I imagine it this way in part because I put it there. My father died on November 25, 1988, at five in the morning, at Evanston Hospital, Evanston, Illinois, a month after he had a stroke on the Dan Ryan Expressway, and I, as one of his two closest living relatives, consented to an autopsy.

There was nothing unusual about my father's death. It was not a medical mystery. He'd had, as one of the residents put it, "a major bleed." To paraphrase another, he'd suffered a medical insult. Or, as he himself said when I entered his cubicle in the emergency room, *I had a strake*, which felt, as I saw him slipping, no less than that the gods of fate had driven a stake through his heart. There followed a craniotomy, tracheotomy, pulmonary embolism, mucus plug, brain death, pneumonia. But when, four weeks later, in the light of early morning, the attending physician asked, as part of the routine postmortem protocol, about an autopsy, I felt what I can only call, even after these many years, a twinge of hope. My father was dead, but maybe the autopsy would explain it.

* * *

The pathologist-cum-essayist F. Gonzalez Crussi, writing about autopsy, talks about "the familiar Y-shaped incision," and I feel a catch in my breathing. Familiar to whom?

Like a would-be scientist I entertain thoughts of discovery, causes, the seat of disease; but like the daughter I really am, I blanch at the flash of a blade, the whir of a saw.

Autopsy is a dissection—an invasion—of the human body. If I didn't know that then, I know it now.

Then, five-fifteen, five-thirty, the hospital corridor dim, dawn not yet breaking, a bleary-eyed doctor asked if we would consent to an autopsy. It was part of his job, his checklist. There were four of us. My brother Gary, his girlfriend Jill, Ann, me. We were children, all of us, and unaccustomed to making these decisions. We had spent the night at the Holiday Inn, not wanting to leave the hospital, not wanting to stay, a limbo night, awaiting one man's death. We'd asked the nurse to call us when it was time.

* * *

The Holiday Inn looked more like a parking garage than a hotel. The front entrance seemed like the back. The four of us were almost giddy. Two siblings and their lovers spending the night in a hotel together. Did their parents know? The desk clerk, probably a college student, wore an ill-fitting shirt, a cheap blue tie. I felt like we were pulling something over on him. At the same time, I wanted to include him in our conspiracy. Our father's in the hospital, I told him, nodding toward my brother. We're expecting a phone call. The clerk looked frightened, a little confused; or maybe that's how I wanted him to look.

We got a double double, and charged it on American Express. None of us even had a toothbrush. A placard on the dresser suggested we call the front desk if we forgot something—toothpaste, a razor—but none of us did. Ann and I heard rustling from the other bed; clothes flung on the floor. This is weird, one of us said.

* * *

We arrived back in the room for my father's last half hour of breathing. We surrounded his bed. A man across the hall died too, and they wheeled him out on a gurney, a woman hovering over him. We were all witnesses to the newly dead. I stirred at the offer—it was an offer, wasn't it?—of an autopsy. To help others, the resident suggested. I wasn't interested in others, but I kept that under wraps. I had other motives, murky even to myself. This was solely a seduction of my own making. Jill and Ann demurred; my brother was uncertain. My father was still in his room but not for long. There's no dallying with the dead. I plied Gary's uncertainty; pushed forward; signed the necessary form.

* * *

Somehow I got the impression they called you. After all, we'd embarked on the procedure together, doctor and next of kin, we were coconspirators of sorts, or if not conspirators, explorers, charting the hidden terrain of the human body. I, of course, was the armchair explorer, waiting at home by the telephone, while the doctor, my cohort, was out in the field. But I was the one with the vested interest, the one for whom the results really mattered.

What was taking so long?

Dr. Eller, neurologist, brain surgeon, head honcho, didn't call. Three weeks after the funeral, I left a message with his answering service.

* * *

I own *The Jewish Book of Why*. Its format—a question posed, a question answered—is simple, straightforward. The Jews have been known to be a querying people. Why is blue a Jewish color? "Because the Mediterranean, the largest body of water near ancient Israel, casts a blue hue." Because blue is a "reflection of God's throne, which is believed to be decorated with sapphires." The book itself has a dark-blue cover and flyleaf.

Years later, it is to this source that I turn. It minces no words. "Jewish law forbids mutilating the body." *Kavod ha'met*, the prohibition against the desecration of the dead. My body, the one that reads this, flinches. The afternoon of my father's death, when I told my great-aunt that he was undergoing an autopsy, she said, Cut him up? Never. Her blue eyes, legend in our family, flashed like sapphires.

There are, *The Jewish Book of Why* says, some exceptions. Autopsy is allowed in cases of homicide or where there is suspicion of homicide, and when the findings are *certain* to contribute to the body of medical knowledge. This principle is called *pikkuah nefesh*. Saving a life.

Certain? The criteria are exacting. Daughter or doctor, who would pass muster? Are you ever wrong? I asked Dr. Eller a week before my father's death, when a mucus plug lodged in his throat and stopped his breathing, cutting off oxygen to his brain. Yes, Dr. Eller conceded after a pause—but what daughter, though grasping at whatever straw she could, would fail to hear the unspoken words, *But not about this.*

* * *

1994: my friend N. and I are both orphans. Both in our forties, still children. We talk about our parents. Hers: New Yorkers, sophisticated; her father irascible, opinionated; her mother—on a budget—fashionable. They listened to music. They had a cabin in Upstate New York. My parents: sellers of clothes; dresses, suits, my mother in the showroom, my father on the road; he went to Nebraska, walked through hotel lobbies full of dowagers, only he pronounced it dew-wadge-ers; this before I was born; later, they washed diapers, other people's clothes; they owned and operated a laundromat, my mother talked about the smell of shit. What did I know of them? As a child, my mother tormented a cat by sticking its whiskers up the kitchen faucet. My father, at thirteen, had been to a brothel. There are many facts, but these parents are all dead now.

N. and I talk about how much we want them back. Like good children, we miss them. We bargain. What would we give up to get them back? What would we put on the table? We go straight to the body, our most coveted bargaining chip. Would we give up a leg? The stakes, it seems, are high when bargaining with the dead; a body part for the entire body; no, neither of us would give up a limb. What about a hand, a foot, then? Would you relinquish that? We look at each other. Our eyes film over; our voices waver. We love them, we miss them. Each of us, we're remembering; our whole lives pass before us. But no, if the price is a hand or a foot, we would not pay it. We shrug our shoulders. We want to remain intact. Nervously we laugh. This is ridiculous, but does that stop us? Okay, then, one of us continues, the test apparently not over, what about a finger? Would you give up a finger to get one of your parents back? Each of us looks inward. I do not know what she sees inside, but it does not take us long to answer. Not even a finger, it turns out, would we give up to get our parents back. Not one single digit.

* * *

I have in my possession my father's death certificate. I dig it out of a plastic bag filled with other accountings: birthday cards my father saved and dated; legal papers authorizing his name change from Shinitzky to Shinner; something called the "Ten Commandments of a Winner," homespun homilies to shore yourself up with when you stand in front of the mirror wondering who you are and what you've become. "A WINNER says 'I'm good, but not as good as I ought to be.' A loser says 'I'm not as bad as other people.'"

Issued before the autopsy, the death certificate is a document brimming with possibility. I know what it says, but I'm sure it says more. It's layered, if only I could read it. Part of its power lies in the fact that it remains. It stands in his stead. *Nathan Shinner. Male. White. American*. An incomplete rendering is better than none at all. This is an official document; a certificate; a ceremony on paper. He was the son of Anna and Isadore. He served in World War II. He made his living in the furniture business. On the lower right-hand corner, the certificate is embossed with a seal that looks like an emblem or crown. The state notices your comings and goings. It takes an interest. The original is filed with the Office of Vital Records in Springfield, the state capital.

I study this piece of paper, which is, I tell myself when I feel the need for the leveling effect of reality, a photocopy. I've come back to it again and again. My father died of (a) bronchopneumonia, due to or as a consequence of (b) illegible, due to or as a consequence of (c) intracerebral hemorrhage, (c) being the last and underlying cause, the certificate says, and the first of the insults. It's signed by one C. Laurie Brown, Local Registrar, who, in a slanted, authoritative signature, certifies that "the foregoing is a true and correct copy of the death record for the decedent," whom she certainly never met.

* * *

A month after my father died, I got together with his younger sister, Zelda, in a kosher pizza parlor on Devon. We were not close. There'd been a longstanding battle over my father that probably began forty years earlier—the day he left the apartment above his family's dry cleaning store and married my long-waisted, melancholy mother—and had surfaced yet again at his shiva when Zelda, Orthodox, argued with the rabbi, Reform and chosen by my brother and me, about the rabbi's right to assemble a minyan and preside over my father's passing. This was more than a theological parting, two branches of Judaism duking it out in one diminished family; this was, at its very root, proprietary. *Who owns this man?* Who, among his survivors, shall stake their claim and secure the body? Zelda had left my father's house that night, gone back to her own, and for the rest of the week, placed her couch cushion on the floor and sat shiva there. At the restaurant, both my parents dead now, she was going to lay it all out.

I ordered a slice of mushroom pizza, the rubbery disks toppled from a can. Even though it was winter, Zelda drank iced tea. She looked like my grandmother, who, when my father—firstborn, beloved son—was drafted into the army, tried to kill herself: gray bristly hair, eyelids folded like draperies, a jaw that might have been excavated. Her voice had the same yawing energy. Do you know about Margie? she said, wiping a napkin over her profuse lips. My father might as well have been served up on the table between us.

Margie? That Gentile name, so like my own, sounded like a recrimination.

In that dung-colored restaurant, Zelda was lit up. You think he's so good but I know better, she flung across the table. I tried to ward her off, protest that of course he wasn't perfect, making reference to his argumentative nature, his capacity for meanness, as if I were admitting to my own faults, but my efforts were useless. Grief had vitalized her, given her an added edge. She would wipe out my father as I knew him, and replace him with a version of her own. She plunked her arms down and proceeded.

The facts were few and simple. My father dated Margie after the war, before your mother, Zelda made it a point to add, in order, it seemed, to preempt her. Margie wasn't Jewish. He got her pregnant. There was a baby. A boy. Here Zelda paused, and in the momentary silence that filled the space between us, the baby materialized before me, life-size and squirming.

He paid all the medical expenses, she said, but beyond that she had no idea what had happened to either of them, Margie or the baby, nor did she know the baby's name. All she remembered, as she delivered this news across the table, was the name of the obstetrician; and all I remember, as I write this years later, is not the obstetrician's name, which I looked up once in the phone book and have since, regretfully, forgotten, but the name of the baby, the name I gave the baby, slapped on as he appeared that day in front of me, sudden and unexpected, at the kosher pizza place on Devon, slick from the labor of his birth: Little Marvin.

Little Marvin? This half-brother, at least four years older, has always been a baby to me, his gestation complete over the course of one lunchtime and his growth terminated during that same meal as well. I try to imagine him as a man but he turns fuzzy, and I prefer to keep him as a newborn. Or he becomes too real, his paunch overhanging his pants, his face dark and stubbly, needing a shave; better the soft-skinned, milk-fed face of an infant. He appeared soon after my father had died, and, I suppose, just like my father, he'll live on indefinitely, haunting the fringes.

* * *

In hospitals, there are hierarchies of waiting. The day lounge, the surgery lounge, the intensive-care family room—in each you wait anxiously longer, because the procedures you are waiting to hear about are increasingly invasive and complex. Once I waited with my mother, for her mother to come out of surgery. My mother was dying of thyroid cancer, but nobody was ready to admit that yet. As we sat in the waiting room—the clock reminding you that the doctor had said surgery would take three hours, and now it's been four—my mother told me about a woman she'd recently heard about who had parked her car by some railroad tracks and walked in front of a train. Do you feel like a train is coming? I wanted to ask but couldn't.

And while we're waiting? They're cutting the body open. That objectified mass of muggers (don't they, in a dark corner of our imagination, put something over our loved one's face to knock her or him out?) and cutters and slicers to whom we've entrusted our parent, child, lover, or friend. First they numb it, a part of it or the whole, and then, tools in hand, they make the cut. Scalpels, forceps, hemostats, clamps, retractors, drills, saws, sutures, staples, swabs, sponges, scissors, scopes, lasers. The list of instruments, to the uninitiated, is staggering and often arcane. Some are frighteningly familiar—the saw—and others, like the surgical robotic arm (one model is named da Vinci), the latest in modern technology. How many of us have not seen a TV representation of an operating room, *Dr. Kildare*, *Marcus Welby*, *ER*, *Scrubs*: the raised gloved hands, the sterile scrubs, the monitors, the tray of gleaming instruments, and the doctor, hovering over the covered, recumbent, sedated body, turning a fraction toward the nurse, extending a hand and bidding "Scalpel"?

Informed consent. That's the covenant binding most surgeries: we want to be cured, we want to be fixed. But at its root, its most elementary, consent is consent to cut. Permission to come in and have a look. It's not permission lightly given, or, says essayist Richard Selzer, himself a surgeon, easily received. In a sense, surgery breaks a taboo against seeing into the body. "I feel [an] . . . irrational fear that it is an evil deed for which punishment awaits. Consider. The sight of our internal organs is denied us. To how many men is it given to look upon their own spleens, their hearts, and live?"

When they opened up my father's brain after the stroke, to relieve the swelling, they said, I waited in the intensive-care family lounge with Ann and friends. There were cartons of Chinese food from the Pineyard. The television was on: home shopping. Down some corridor, past some outsize metal doors, in a theater brightly lit, the neurosurgeon and his crew picked and probed. Past the skull, the dura mater, into the cerebral cortex—the seat of movement and speech and thought—the doctors would see what neither my father nor I had ever seen before, and they would see it not in a picture or on a screen but in the actual living flesh. They would seal off the ruptured vessel, clean out the blood. Then, when they were done, they would close him up.

* * *

In the seventies I volunteered briefly at the Emma Goldman Women's Health Center, a storefront clinic that advocated a woman's control over her own body—her sexual and reproductive organs—but I always felt like an impostor. I could never quite get the hang of it, putting in the speculum, getting the cervix into view, holding up the mirror. I was clumsy, and not quite enthused. And once I managed to accomplish all this maneuvering, what, exactly, was I seeing? I would put the discharge on a slide and place it under the microscope, as I'd seen the other health-care workers do, but I couldn't identify the shapes that seemed to shift under my unsteady gaze. Still, I kept at it for almost a year, because I liked going to the biweekly meetings, where we argued whether doctors were necessary.

Ann, however, had steered clear of the self-help movement. Jokingly, but not a joke, she says that maybe there was a reason we'd never looked inside before, kept ourselves hidden, a reason beyond the conspiracy of doctors, mostly male, who presumed to know more than we did. She, for one, had had little desire to insert a speculum and see her cervix reflected in a mirror, and her disclaimer now, years later, is accompanied by a shudder. Is this a distancing from our bodies so complete that all we can do is shudder in response, or is this respectful, proper distance, an innate recognition that some things are better left unseen? Look within, we tell ourselves in times of self-assessment, but that is metaphorical.

* * *

Once I saw a video of the body's insides. It was part of a one-woman show by Palestinian artist Mona Hatoum at the Museum of Contemporary Art. I entered a dark, curtained cubicle, not knowing what to expect, and watched a continuous-loop video showing the sinewy trails of Hatoum's innards. There was the squish and glisten of organs, a sense of pulsing and jostling, a moist display of orange viscera. Sound accompanied the video: bubbling, belching. In the darkness of the cubicle, I had the impression of being surrounded. Skin, the protective filter, had been removed, the skeleton as well, and I was immersed in the body. This was the life within the life, the body we often take for granted. Hatoum's body, but it could have been anyone's.

* * *

On my driver's license, next to my picture, it says DONOR. I've agreed to be an organ donor. I agreed to this when I renewed my license, on my fifty-first birthday. The back of my license informs me that THIS IS A LEGAL DOCUMENT UNDER THE UNIFORM ANATOMICAL GIFT ACT. I see, however, now that I look, that I haven't signed the form. I haven't indicated if my whole body is ripe for the taking, or only certain specified organs. You get to parcel yourself out if you want. *Take my cornea, fine, my kidneys too, but please, not my heart.* Is the document legal without a signature? Is it binding?

Ann and I went to renew our licenses together. When they asked if she wanted to become a donor, she said yes. I did too. But I agreed because she did. I followed her lead. I didn't want to be thought of as ungenerous, although I don't think Ann would think of me that way. Ann loves me because of, not in spite of, who I am. I guess I felt, in some cosmic appraisal of my own devising, I would fall short. The pressure's on to be an organ donor. The ad campaign says it's the gift of life. (Or is that blood? I have, for the record, given blood.) Who could refuse? Former Chicago Bears running back Walter Payton died because there wasn't a liver available when he needed one. He was an affable guy with a high-pitched voice and a prankster's sense of humor. At forty-five, he was the fallen athlete. I was moved by his death, not only because it came too soon, but because his descent, from heights far greater than the rest of us will likely attain, was so precipitous. As an organ donor I could help someone like him and, added bonus, pat myself on the back in anticipation of doing so.

The unsigned license is a reproach, but I make no move to sign it. Alone and unobserved, I casually demur. I'm nonchalant about it, as though it's an oversight I might eventually correct. Jews give money, I suddenly say to myself, not organs. When a person dies, we give to a charitable organization in his or her name. As proof I make a quick perusal of the *New York Times*: in lieu of flowers (Jews don't give flowers either), donations can be made to the Ronald

McDonald House, the Multiple Sclerosis Foundation, Hadassah, the Alzheimer's Foundation, et cetera, et cetera. Never mind that my assertion echoes similar ones my father used to make, assertions that had infuriated me with their blind, dismissive, self-congratulatory virtue. *Jews don't drink, Jews don't beat their wives*, and now, apparently, in continuation of that same line of thinking, Jews don't give organs.

So here I am, a hypocrite: invoking my religion when I don't practice it, signing up to be an organ donor when I don't mean it. Profligate at times with my money, it seems that with my own homegrown resource I'm a miser. I'm not sure I want to go to my grave—and I do want a grave; I want visitors to leave stones on my marker—parceled out. I feel loyal to my body. It is, for better and for worse, for all its betrayals and my abuses, mine. I imagine a final leave-taking, when death comes, and body and soul part ways: Bye-bye, the soul might say to the body. Bye-bye, the body, shrugged off and discarded now, replies. It's been quite a ride, both agree. They embrace, one last conjoining. Take care. Be well. Have a good flight.

And the soul takes off. And the body is at rest.

* * *

The body, of course, is penetrated by sex. There we are, wagging penises, tongues, fingers, fists, dildos. Various objects, human and otherwise, seek and gain entry. My friend N.'s sister was an STD nurse in California, and reported a whole range of objects she and her medical colleagues had to remove from the orifices of the human body, placed there for some giddy mixture of pleasure, intimacy, experiment, cruelty, and humor. It seems we have the urge to enter, gain access, grant and be granted right-of-way.

I spent an afternoon thumbing through an anatomy textbook. I was looking for a picture that would show everything, the whole works, all the body's parts and connections. What I found instead were systems—the skeletal system, the circulatory system, the gastrointestinal tract—each one frustratingly barring me from another, a series of looping cul-de-sacs. Somehow, I'd likened the body to a structure with a shell; I thought that if I cracked it open, I would get to the center, the very core.

But, I reminded myself, I'd already been inside. As a onetime graduate student in exercise physiology, I'd taken a human anatomy course dissecting cadavers. I'd cut open the human body, picked apart those systems, held a coiled small intestine in my hand. There is no center, no core, not anatomically at least, not like I was looking for—a homunculus pulling the strings, an internal puppeteer. The center? *Is that the soul?* a voice inside me asks, and that selfsame voice answers, *I don't know.*

History is full of philosophers and theologians, as well as pedestrian fellow travelers such as myself, whose quest for the soul—or something like it—has led, among other sites, to the liver, the heart, the brain. I've held those in my hand as well. I've correctly identified them in a final exam. The ancient Babylonians, who considered the liver the seat of the soul, consulted a sheep's liver before going into battle, for help divining the course of the future. The Japanese have long located the soul in the lower abdomen. The practice of ritual suicide, hara kiri, literally means to cut open the abdomen and release the soul. In my martial arts practice, we speak of moving from your *hara*, your center—your little rice cooker, as I once heard it called—located several inches below the navel. The French, who have elevated the liver to a place of great importance, if not the site of the soul, refer to an overall feeling of unwellness as *mal de foie.*

But the heart and the brain remain the two main contenders. Ancient Egyptians weighed a person's heart after death, because they believed its weight equaled that of the soul, the two, in their view, being inextricable. Aristotle said that the pneuma, or vital spirit, came directly from the heavens and was distributed throughout the body by the heart, the seat of the soul. The heart has a language of its own, suggesting some deep place, some all-encompassing entirety of being: *heartfelt, heartsick, take to heart, learn by heart, eat your heart out.* After my father died, I developed a pain in my chest, a heaviness that felt like a stone, which my doctor, after putting away her stethoscope, suggested might be heartache.

Descartes, notwithstanding his countrymen's affection for the liver, argued that God placed the soul in the brain: *Cogito ergo sum; I think, therefore I am.* Is that why, I wonder, when Americans, American men at least, commit suicide, they often go right to the source, and blow their brains out? Women, in my unscientific observations, prefer methods involving less cleanup. My friend S. scoffs at this idea, maintaining that people blow their brains out because it works.

What does all this prove? That the soul is a wily creature? That it can't be pinned down? *My father's brain is in a jar.* I think of it sitting there, on the shelf in Evanston Hospital, where, in my imagination at least, I have placed it; and while I'm not so literal as to believe his soul is trapped inside, I can't help feeling that perhaps some essence is squeezed within that clear, contoured glass, some vital distillation, something that made him Nathan Shinner, formerly Shinitzky, charming, funny, loyal, my father.

* * *

Finally Dr. Eller called with the results of the autopsy, more than three weeks after my father's death. I remember his uneasiness, as if he were as disconcerted relaying the results of an autopsy, on the phone, to the daughter of the deceased as I was hearing them. He went through his list. My father had advanced arteriosclerosis, he said, and immediately I felt upset, taken aback, as if my father were alive and, up until now, healthy—and not, in fact, dead from one of the corollaries of this very condition—and we were receiving the diagnosis for the first time, a diagnosis that would, from here on out, forever change his life. There was no sign of the stomach cancer he'd been treated for two years previous, Dr. Eller continued. Distraught at hearing the diagnosis of arteriosclerosis, I was almost blasé to find out he'd had no recurrence of stomach cancer. As if I expected it; of course he didn't have stomach cancer; he'd beaten it. We found a cancerous mass in the bladder, Dr. Eller said. Cancer of the bladder? Something lying in wait to kill my father—another cancer no less, which seemed unfair, as if a person should not be made to suffer more than one malignancy—if he hadn't been killed by a stroke instead?

But none of this explained my father's death. None of this explained why he died when he died, at 5:00 a.m., on November 25, 1988. Did I want to know what happened so I could have prevented it from happening, just as I had tried to stave off all the events of those preceding four weeks, the brain swelling, brain surgery, tracheotomy, pulmonary embolism, as if by will and love and bedside vigilance I, and I alone, could have altered the course of his condition, or was I casting a question, a plea, up to the heavens? Why did he die? As for the immediate cause of death, Dr. Eller said, we're still examining his brain but have found nothing conclusive.

Examining his brain? My voice cracked in disbelief. My father, according to Jewish tradition, had been buried expeditiously, he died on a Friday and was buried the next Monday, but they, the doctors, were now, three weeks later, examining his brain. Which meant his brain, to put it indelicately—but is there any other way to put it, for it struck me with blunt, brutal force—was not in his head. Of course, you may say—you, who are reading this (already picturing his brain in a jar), you, that other part of myself who has been wrestling with this ever since—but I didn't know that. I didn't know that an autopsy meant removing organs and not putting them back. I pictured it, if I pictured it at all, as a quick little look-see, a tidy examination: peruse the premises, snip a few tissues here and there, samples to put under the microscope, and then zipper him back up again, untampered, unmolested, everything intact. I didn't expect him to be excavated, for his skull to be scooped clean.

* * *

Since then the years have added up. It is now, again, the season of my father's death. Outside the window, the grass is green and yellow and brown, and the trees are almost, but not quite, leafless. A bird with tattered tail feathers has just stopped on the window ledge to rest. Every year I light a candle to commemorate my father's death, a candle that, even though I buy it at the Jewel in the Kosher-style foods section, comes alive for me, and I stupidly sing, to myself or to Ann, *This little light of mine, I'm going to let it shine*, and the candle burns for twenty-four hours. I have as well in these years kept alive my guilt—kept it alive, I realize now, gladly and energetically, with dedication. I've read some of what Jewish law says about autopsies, and little bits and pieces from other religions too, and I feel vindicated, not when I find opinions in favor of autopsy, but when I find interpretations against it. A leading rabbinical authority writes, "an autopsy is warranted only . . . for purposes of deriving specific information deemed essential for the treatment of another patient already suffering the same illness, [but not] in the *vague* hope [emphasis mine] that medical knowledge may be . . . enriched," and though part of me blanches at the pure miserliness of this statement, at its unforgivably snide tone (the kind of thing, I hear the accumulated history of anti-Semitism saying, that gives Jews a bad name), another part of me latches on to it as confirmation. *See*, I say to the jury my mind's hastily corralled for the purpose of registering blame. *See*, I say to myself.

* * *

My father and I had a ritual. When he wanted to be affectionate, he would take his fist, which looked enormous to me, and slowly but firmly push it into my cheek while I, in a reciprocating gesture, pushed back. We kept pushing until we reached a point of equal tension, fist to cheek. Then, gently, we released. We did this in the car, stopped at a light, when I was the driver and he was in the passenger's seat so, I suspect, we could avoid eye contact. I kept my eye on traffic; I don't know where he kept his.

I consented to the autopsy because I wanted to know why he died. But I wasn't, as it turned out—as it turned out in the aftermath of the autopsy—asking a medical question, I wasn't looking for scientific causes and effects. My father had a stroke—an intracerebral hemorrhage, a major bleed—on the Dan Ryan Expressway, and four weeks later he died. That's the cause, and the effect. I was asking the gods a question, a child's question about her father, one anyone might ask; but in my confusion I went to the wrong source, I went to the gods of medicine when I should have been beseeching the ever-present gods of fate.

Does he blame me? He was, he could be, a vindictive person. The kind of guy who held a grudge. He'd been under the knife a number of times in the last years of his life, and I'd put him under again. What would he say to me? What would he say to me now? Now Ann pushes her fist against my cheek (over the years she's picked this up), but unlike my father and me, we look at each other and smile. Her hand is smaller than his, but no less tender, and I meet it, pushing back. Then I put the car in gear and we drive off.

My father doesn't say anything. He doesn't let me off the hook, and he doesn't point a finger at me either. He is, and has been, forever silent on this point. That leaves it up to me. The next time I pay him a visit, I'll tear off a few blades of grass, gather some pebbles, and scatter them all on his grave.

Acknowledgments

Thank you to Leslie Walker Williams, my ever-willing reader, for her sharp commentary and sturdy friendship. Thank you to Sandi Wisenberg for taking a turn at these essays yet again, and for being in my corner. Thank you to Rosellen Brown and Nora Dvosin for tackling the order of the essays, to Rosellen, fairy godmother extraordinaire, for opening the door, and to Nora for meals across the table in Dixon; to my writing group, Garnett Kilberg-Cohen, Maggie Kast, Rosellen, Sandi, Sharon Solowitz, and Tsivia Cohen, for insightful feedback and ongoing sustenance; and to Michael Martone for giving forth with kindness and generosity.

I am grateful to the late Jeanne Leiby of the *Southern Review* for phoning out of the blue and to my agent, Ayesha Pande, for standing by the writer as well as the book. Thanks to University of Chicago Press executive editor Susan Bielstein for bringing these essays on a road trip, to her collaborator, Anthony Burton, for his calm counsel, and to Sandra Hazel for her sensitive guidance.

Thanks to Ragdale, the Ucross Foundation, and Ausable Press for time, solitude, and vistas. Thanks also to the Illinois Arts Council for generous support; to the Leopold and Loeb Collection at the Charles Deering McCormick Library of Special Collections at Northwestern University for access to materials; and to Bridget Canavan for research assistance.

Gratitude to Amy Blumenthal, Ann Christophersen, Betsy Williams, Candace Chaite, Jean Hardisty, Julia Voss, Marie O'Brien, Mark Saxe, Martha Thompson, Megan Carney, Michal Eskayo, Nancy Lanoue, and Sarah Ludden for their support of this book and the plenty of friendship; to my brother, Gary, who reminded me, *You are your own memento;* and to my teachers and training partners at Thousand Waves Martial Arts & Self-Defense Center for years of everyday courage.

In memory of my parents, Harriet Shinner, née Alter, and Nathan Shinner, formerly Shinitzky, and of my great-aunt, Etta Fefferman, who once famously said, *Never go to bed angry.*

And to Ann Tyler, for thirty-six years and all the inestimables.

Thanks also to the publications in which earlier versions of these essays appeared:

"Family Feet," *Southern Review* 45, no. 1 (Winter 2009): 95–107.

"Pocketing," *Alaska Quarterly Review* 28, nos. 3 and 4 (Fall–Winter 2011): 61–70.

"The Knife," *Bloom* 2, no. 1 (Spring 2005): 137–51.

"Elective," Chicago issue, *ACM/Another Chicago Magazine* 1, no. 50 (2010): 131–44.

"The Fitting(s)," *New Delta Review* 27 (2010): 100–112.

"Berenice's Hair," *Southern Review* 47, no. 3 (Summer 2011): 446–49.

"Leopold and Shinner," *Colorado Review* 37, no. 3 (Fall–Winter 2010): 76–94.

"Tax Time," in *The Oldest We've Ever Been: Seven True Stories of Midlife Transitions*, edited by Maud Lavin, 132–40 (Tucson: University of Arizona Press, 2008). © 2008 The Arizona Board of Regents. Reprinted by permission of the University of Arizona Press.

"Mood Medicine," *Gettysburg Review* 20, no. 3 (Autumn 2007): 467–74.

"Post-Mortem," *Fourth Genre: Explorations in Nonfiction* 9, no. 1 (Spring 2007): 131–44. Published by Michigan State University Press.

"Post-Mortem," excerpted as "A Leg, a Hand, a Foot, a Finger," *ACM/Another Chicago Magazine*, no. 37 (2000): 186–87.